Beginning Android Programming

DEVELOP AND **DESIGN**

**Kevin Grant and
Chris Haseman**

PEACHPIT PRESS
WWW.PEACHPIT.COM

Beginning Android Programming: Develop and Design

Kevin Grant and Chris Haseman

Peachpit Press

www.peachpit.com

To report errors, please send a note to errata@peachpit.com
Peachpit Press is a division of Pearson Education.

Copyright © 2014 by Kevin Grant and Chris Haseman

Editor: Clifford Colby
Development editor: Robyn Thomas
Production editor: Danielle Foster
Copyeditor: Scout Festa
Technical editors: Matthew Brochstein and Vijay Penemetsa
Cover design: Aren Straiger
Interior design: Mimi Heft
Compositor: Danielle Foster
Indexer: Valerie Haynes Perry

ISBN-13: 978-0-321-95656-9
ISBN-10:   0-321-95656-7

9 8 7 6 5 4 3 2 1

Printed and bound in the United States of America

To my love, Erica, who's encouraged me to dream bigger than I've ever imagined; my mother, J'nette, who is my best friend and biggest fan; and my grandmother, Helene, who always supported me in all of my endeavors.

—Kevin Grant

ACKNOWLEDGMENTS

As always, I could spend more pages thanking people than are in the work itself. Here are a few who stand out:

Cliff C. for getting me on board (and always letting me know the weather). Robyn T. for her diligence in keeping us all on time, and deleting all of my superfluous words. Scout F. for her tolerance of my grammar. Matthew B. for helping out while taking care of his new baby boy. Vijay P. for coming in under a tight deadline and working till the end. The mobile team at Tumblr for their encouragement (cleverly disguised as snark). The Android team at Google for building great new tools and making every release feel like a birthday. Most of all, Peachpit for giving me the opportunity to write for you.

ABOUT THE AUTHORS

Kevin Grant is an Android Engineer at Tumblr, a creative blogging platform in New York City, where he focuses on application design, implementing the latest design paradigms, and pushing the boundaries of the Android framework.

He began developing for Android in 2009, performing research at the University of Nevada, Reno. After graduating, he was employed in Malmö, Sweden, where he further honed his mobile skills in the Scandinavian startup scene.

Chris Haseman has been writing mobile software in various forms since 2003. He was involved in several large projects, from MMS messaging to Major League Baseball. More recently, he was an early Android engineer behind the doubleTwist media player and is now the Engineering Manager for the Mobile team at Tumblr. He lives in Manhattan with his wife, Meghan, and constantly debates shaving his beard.

CONTENTS

INTRODUCTION

If you've got a burning idea for an application that you're dying to share, or if you recognize the power and possibilities of the Android platform, you've come to the right place. This is a short book on an immense topic.

We don't mean to alarm anyone right off the bat here, but let's be honest: Android development is hard. Its architecture is dissimilar to that of many existing platforms (especially other mobile SDKs), there are many traps for beginners to fall into, and you might find yourself running to the Internet for answers. In exchange for its difficulty, however, Google's Android offers unprecedented power, control, and—yes—responsibility to those who are brave enough to develop for it.

This is where our job comes in. We're here to make the process of learning to write amazing Android software as simple as possible.

Who are we to ask such things of you? Chris Haseman has been writing mobile software in a professional capacity for ten years, and for five of those years, he's been developing software for Android. He's also written code that runs on millions of handsets throughout the world. Also, he has a beard. We all know that people with ample facial hair appear to be more authoritative on all subjects.

Kevin Grant has been developing for Android since its inception and has worked on a breadth of user-facing products, developing beautiful and intuitive interfaces for millions of users. While he doesn't have a beard, we all know that people with a perpetual five o'clock shadow know how to get things done.

From here on out, we're going to take this conversation into the first person. We banter enough amongst ourselves—it's not necessary to confuse you in the process. So without further ado, in return for making this learning process as easy as possible, I ask for a few things:

- **You have a computer.** My third-grade teacher taught me never to take anything for granted; maybe you *don't* have a computer. If you don't already have a computer, you'll need one—preferably a fast one, because the Android emulator and Eclipse can use up a fair amount of resources quickly.

NOTE: Android is an equal-opportunity development platform. While I personally develop on a Mac, you can use any of the three major platforms (Mac, PC, or Linux).

- **You're fluent in Java.** Notice that I say *fluent,* not *expert.* Because you'll be writing usable applications (rather than production libraries, at least to start), I expect you to know the differences between classes and interfaces. You should be able to handle threads and concurrency without batting an eyelash. Further, the more you know about what happens under the hood (in terms of object creation and garbage collection), the faster and better your mobile applications will be.

Yes, you can get through the book and even put together rudimentary applications without knowing much about the Java programming language. However, when you encounter problems—in both performance and possibilities—a weak foundation in the programming language may leave you without a solution.

- **You have boundless patience and endless curiosity.** Your interest in and passion for Android will help you through the difficult subjects covered in this book and let you glide through the easy ones.

Throughout this book, I focus on how to write features, debug problems, and make interesting software. I hope that when you've finished the book, you'll have a firm grasp of the fundamentals of Android software development.

All right, that's quite enough idle talking. Let's get started.

> **NOTE:** If you're more interested in the many "whys" behind Android, this book is a good one to start with, but it won't answer every question you may have.

WHO THIS BOOK IS FOR

This book is for people who have some programming experience and are curious about the wild world of Android development.

WHO THIS BOOK IS NOT FOR

This book is not for people who have never seen a line of Java before. It is also not for expert Android engineers with several applications under their belt.

HOW YOU WILL LEARN

In this book, you'll learn by doing. Each chapter comes with companion sample code and clear, concise instructions for how to build that code for yourself. You'll find the code samples on the book's website (www.peachpit.com/androiddevelopanddesign).

WHAT YOU WILL LEARN

You'll learn the basics of Android development, from creating a project to building scalable UIs that move between tablets and phones.

WELCOME TO ANDROID

Eclipse and Android Studio are the two supported integrated development environments (IDEs) for Android development, and you need only one to follow along with the examples in this book. There are, however, a few other tools you should be aware of that will be very useful now and in your future work with Android. While you may not use all these tools until you're getting ready to ship an application, it will be helpful to know about them when the need arises.

ECLIPSE (ADT BUNDLE)

Eclipse was the first publicly available IDE for Android and has been in use since 2008. Previous iterations required a complicated setup process that involved downloading multiple pieces and duct-taping them together. Now, with the debut of ADT Bundle, the process is much easier. Everything you need to build an Android application in Eclipse is in one convenient bundle, preconfigured to get you up and running in under five minutes.

ANDROID STUDIO

A spinoff of the popular Java IDE Intellij, Android Studio is Google's newest solution to many of our Android development woes. With Android Studio, Android receives a new unified build system, Gradle, which is fully integrated to allow the utmost flexibility in your development process. It may be a little rough around the edges, and it may take a little extra elbow grease, but you'll find that the time invested will pay off in the long run.

ANDROID SDK

The Android SDK contains all the tools you'll need to develop Android applications from the command line, as well as other tools that will help you find and diagnose problems and streamline your applications. Whether you use Eclipse or Android Studio, the Android SDK comes preconfigured and is identical for both IDEs.

ANDROID SDK MANAGER

The Android SDK Manager (found within the SDK tools/ directory) will help you pull down all versions of the SDK, as well as a plethora of tools, third-party add-ons, and all things Android. This will be the primary way in which you get new software from Google's headquarters in Mountain View, California.

ANDROID VIRTUAL DEVICE MANAGER

Android Virtual Device Manager is for those developers who prefer to develop on an emulator rather than an actual device. It's a little slow, but you can run an Android emulator for any version of Android, at any screen size. It's perfect for testing screen sizes, screen density, and operating system versions across a plethora of configurations.

HIERARCHY VIEWER

This tool will help you track the complex connections between your layouts and views as you build and debug your applications. This viewer can be indispensable when tracking down those hard-to-understand layout issues. You can find this tool in the SDK tools/ directory as hierarchyviewer.

MONITOR

Also known as DDMS (Dalvik Debug Monitor Server), Monitor is your primary way to interface with and debug Android devices. You'll find it in the tools/ directory inside the Android SDK. It does everything from gathering logs, sending mock text messages or locations, and mapping memory allocations to taking screenshots. This tool is very much the Swiss Army knife of your Android toolkit. Along with being a standalone application, both Eclipse and Android Studio users can access this tool from directly within their programs.

GRADLE

This is the new build system in Android Studio. The beauty of Gradle is that whether you press "Build" from within the IDE or build from the command line, you are building with the same system. For general use, there aren't many commands you will need to know, but I cover basic and advanced Gradle usage at the end of the book.

CHAPTER 1

Getting Started with Android

The first and arguably most pivotal step to building an Android application is installing an integrated development environment (IDE). If you've already built an Android application and are comfortable with the IDE you chose—Eclipse (ADT Bundle) or Android Studio—congratulations are in order! You can skip this chapter and move on to the fundamentals. For those of you who haven't, you'll get through this before you can say "Open Handset Alliance" three times quickly.

In this chapter, you'll move quickly through the platform configuration. You'll

- Learn about your IDE options
- Download and configure Eclipse (ADT Bundle) or Android Studio
- Update the Android software development kit (SDK) to the latest version
- Create and configure a shiny new Android emulator
- Start a new Android project
- Run your Android project on your shiny new Android emulator
  Excited yet?

EXPLORING ANDROID DEVELOPMENT ENVIRONMENTS

So you have to make a decision, beyond the decision to read this book! The decision is between Eclipse (ADT Bundle) and Android Studio. You're free to change your mind at any point during the book, and if you're really ambitious, you might even choose both. It's important to understand a few key differences between these IDEs before deciding.

ECLIPSE (ADT BUNDLE)

Android's home and birthplace. Formerly, Android users needed to download a standalone version of Eclipse and configure the Android software development kit (we'll just call it SDK from here on out) separately. Google has alleviated all this hassle by packaging the SDK with Eclipse and branding it as ADT Bundle. Eclipse has been Android's primary development environment since its preview release in 2008. Since then, just about every Android app that you know and love (or hate) has been built in Eclipse. It has wonderful strengths, its setup gets easier with every iteration, and there are years of amazing source code, project trouble-shooting, and development guides all over the Internet that are exclusively linked to it.

Pros:

- Up and running in less than 5 minutes.
- Most open-source projects from 2008 to 2013 are designed to be imported into Eclipse.
- Every problem you could ever have with Android and Eclipse has been asked on the Internet 100 times over.

ANDROID STUDIO

Android Studio was announced at Google I/O 2013. It is based on a popular Java IDE named Intellij and is being designed as a complete replacement for Eclipse for developers wanting other options.

Pros:

- Powerful code inspection, capable of understanding how Android resources and source files interact
- Deep integration with Android's new build system, Gradle (more on this later)
- Slated to become the standard Android development tool as adoption grows
- (Bonus!) Dark-themed IDE built in

If you are an experienced Java developer and you are familiar with Intellij, then Android Studio might be for you. However, it is a way less traveled, and you will find yourself with questions that you will have to persevere to figure out. If you have a lot of experience with Eclipse, or no experience at all, then I recommend Eclipse.

GETTING EVERYTHING INSTALLED

Since Eclipse shares many of the same options as Android Studio, it isn't completely necessary to address them in separate chapters. For sections that are pertinent only to one or the other, look for **Eclipse** or **Android Studio** in the title. I promise it's safe to skip over those parts that aren't relevant to your decision.

At this point, there's nothing left to do but get started! If a title doesn't look like it applies to your operating system, skip ahead until you find one that does. Bear with me; you'll be working on your first application in no time.

> **NOTE:** For the duration of this book, I assume you're using Eclipse or Android Studio for most of your development. But I include command-line methods as well as screenshots for all important commands and tasks in case you're rocking the terminal with Vim or Emacs.

INSTALLING ECLIPSE (ADT BUNDLE) FOR OS X, LINUX, WINDOWS

First things first: Whenever I say "Eclipse" in this book, I am referring to ADT Bundle. This is because ADT Bundle is just Eclipse with some extra stuff. With that out of the way, let's get started.

Fire up your favorite Internet browser, and head on over to http://developer.android.com/sdk/index.html. From there, follow the instructions for downloading the appropriate application for your system.

Installing Eclipse is as simple as decompressing the file you've downloaded and putting the application somewhere you'll remember. Although you can unpack this file anywhere, I recommend placing it in /Users/*yourUserName*/Documents/adt-bundle-<distribution-information>/.

Eclipse doesn't install onto your machine like a normal program. The application you see in the unzipped folder is the actual application. Make sure you don't remove Eclipse from that folder; otherwise, Eclipse won't know where to find the Android SDK.

COMMAND-LINE ENTHUSIASTS

If you're using OS X or Linux and you're a command-line person, then I recommend you put two directories on your path, as follows:

1. Navigate to /User/*userName*/.profile.

2. Assuming that you installed the SDK in the location I recommended, add the following code to your profile:

   ```
   export PATH=${PATH}:/Users/<userName>/Documents/adt-bundle/sdk/tools export PATH=${PATH}:/Users/<userName>/Documents/adt-bundle/sdk/platform-tools
   ```

   Now, when you open a new terminal, typing which android will return the path where you installed the Android SDK. Keep this command in mind—you'll return to it in a minute.

INSTALLING ANDROID STUDIO

Go to http://developer.android.com/sdk/installing/studio.html and download the appropriate file for your system. Browser operating system detection is pretty great nowadays, and just by clicking Download you should retrieve the proper application.

OS X

Once you have downloaded the .dmg file for Android Studio from http://developer.android.com/sdk/installing/studio.html, double-click it to open it, and drop the application into your Applications folder.

LINUX

This should be pretty straightforward. Once you have downloaded the .tar file from http://developer.android.com/sdk/installing/studio.html, double-click it to unpack it, and place it in an appropriate location for your distribution.

WINDOWS

On Windows, you are installing an executable instead of just unzipping a folder. After launching the executable that you downloaded from http://developer.android.com/sdk/installing/studio.html, follow the setup wizard for choosing an installation location—that's it!

ISSUES

There are always a few known issues, and Google does a great job of documenting them. Refer to http://tools.android.com/knownissues and look for information related to the issue you're having. Most common issues are based on the system not knowing where the Java Development (JDK) is installed on your system. Android Studio works with JDK 7, but don't download it unless you're sure you need it. And if you've done any development before, you probably already have it.

COMMAND-LINE ENTHUSIASTS

If using OS X or Linux, the command line is invaluable to your Android development process. If ever a time arises that Android Studio is not playing nicely (lookin' at you, Eclipse!), it's generally safe to assume that the command line won't let you down.

1. Navigate to /User/*yourUserName*/.profile.
2. Assuming that you installed the SDK in the Applications folder, add the following code to your profile:

   ```
   export PATH=${PATH}:/Applications/Android\ Studio.app/sdk/tools
   export PATH=${PATH}:/Applications/Android\ Studio.app/sdk/platform-tools
   ```

   Now, when you open a new terminal, typing which android -help will reveal all the tools available to you for managing your SDK and virtual devices.

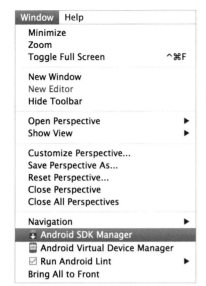

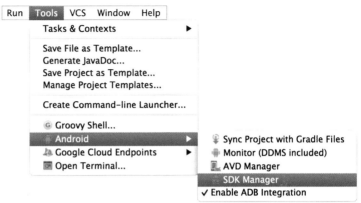

FIGURE 1.1 Locating the SDK Manager in the Eclipse application toolbar

FIGURE 1.2 Locating the SDK Manager in Android Studio

UPDATING THE ANDROID SDK

With your IDE now installed, you're just a few steps away from running your own Android application. You need to update the SDK so that you have options for the emulators you want to use and so that you have source code and resources available for references. By default, your downloaded IDE will have the latest version of the Android SDK packaged with it, but since not all users will always receive the latest and greatest updates, you should download some older SDKs to make sure that all your users are supported.

The first step is to open the SDK Manager.

1. In **Eclipse**, open the ADT Bundle folder you downloaded, and within the `eclipse` folder, double-click to open Eclipse.

   Once it's open, select Window > Android SDK Manager, as in **Figure 1.1**.

   or

   In **Android Studio**, from the application toolbar, choose Tools > Android > SDK Manager (**Figure 1.2**).

   This launches the tool responsible for managing your Android SDK, which includes everything from source files and build tools to Google's add-on libraries, such as in-app billing and application compatibility.

> **TIP:** If you have configured your path properly, you can also access the SDK manager by typing android sdk into the command line (see "Getting Everything Installed").

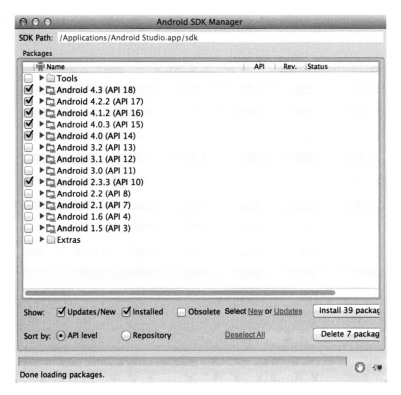

FIGURE 1.3 Downloading Android versions

For many applications, it's not enough to support only the latest version. Unless you know right away which SDK versions you want to support, I recommend selecting the same ones you see selected in **Figure 1.3**:

- Android 2.3.3 (Gingerbread)
- Android 4.0 / 4.0.3 (Ice Cream Sandwich / ICS)
- Android 4.1.x /4.2.x / 4.3.x (Jelly Bean)

By downloading these versions, you should have immediate access to the virtual devices and source files you need to build almost any modern application.

2. In the Android SDK Manager dialog, click Install *x* Packages, agree to Google's terms (read at your own risk), and away you go. This can be a bit tricky because you have to accept each group of licenses individually, so make sure you verify that you've accepted them all.

The Android SDK Manager should download and install the selected platforms for you. This is a large download, so I recommend you do this on a fast and reliable Internet connection.

Keep in mind that the platform you're downloading corresponds to a particular version of the Android operating system running on devices. Older phones may not support all the SDK calls that the latest phones might. As you learn about various SDK calls, you'll learn strategies for dealing with older devices.

CONFIGURING DEVICES

FIGURE 1.4 The Android Virtual Device (AVD) Manager window

With your IDE up and running and your Android SDK up to date, you need to create a device to test your applications on. One of the greatest features of Android development is that you are developing on real devices (or real device emulators). You can have the satisfaction of whipping out your phone and saying "Check out this app I made!" Your friends may not be impressed with your "Hello World" app, but who needs them anyway.

VIRTUAL DEVICE EMULATOR

The virtual device emulator is an application that runs on your computer and completely emulates a real Android device. While this emulation can be a bit slow and the speeds can choke up at times, it is a reliable means of development, and it lets you test on any version of Android without spending a dime. Here's how to create as many virtual devices as your heart desires.

1. With **Eclipse** running, choose Window > Android Virtual Device Manager.

   or

   With **Android Studio** running, choose Tools > Android > AVD Manager.

   or

   If you're a command-line junkie, run android avd in the shell. (I'm going to assume you were able to add it to your path.)

   The Android Virtual Device Manager displays (**Figure 1.4**).

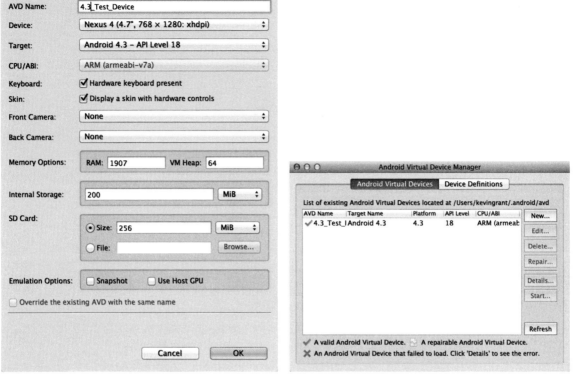

FIGURE 1.5 Android virtual device configuration properties

FIGURE 1.6 Android Virtual Device Manager after creating your first virtual device

2. Click the Android Virtual Devices tab, and click New to open the Create New Android Virtual Device (AVD) dialog.

   Use **Figure 1.5** as a guide to configure your new device.

3. In the AVD Name field, enter a descriptive name, such as "4.3_Test_Device" (allowed characters: numerals, upper- and lowercase letters, period, underscore, and hyphen).

4. Select Nexus 4 from the Device menu.

5. Select Android 4.3 – API Level 18 from the Target menu.

6. In the SD Card field, select the Size radio button and enter **256**.

7. Leave the Snapshot and Use Host GPU options unselected for now; we will address those in a moment.

8. Click OK and do a little dance next to your desk—or don't, it's up to you (**Figure 1.6**).

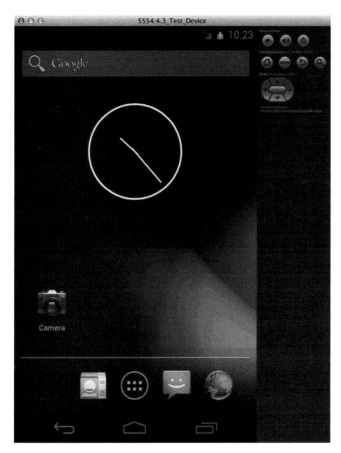

FIGURE 1.7 Your shiny new virtual device!

9. Select your new emulator, and click the Start button to get it running. Feel free to adjust the launch options available to you, but the default ones will be fine for 95 percent of your purposes. Click Launch from the launch options, and the laborious process of spinning up a new instance of the virtual device begins (**Figure 1.7**).

> **TIP:** Once you start an instance of the emulator, you don't ever have to start it up again. Reinstalling the application does not (as it does with many other systems) require you to spawn a new instance of the emulator.

So what about those two options that we left unselected, the Snapshot and Use Host GPU options?

- **Snapshot** saves a snapshot of the device's current state when you close it, making subsequent startups much faster. When this works, it's great! But often you might find that the device was left in a corrupted state and needs to be restarted. When starting the device, look in the launch options window. You'll see two check boxes: Use Launch from Last Snapshot, and Save This Session to a Snapshot. I leave them both selected.

- **Use Host GPU** does what it says—it tries to use the machine's hardware acceleration if and when possible. Refer to http://developer.android.com/tools/devices/emulator.html for more information if you think you need some more horsepower.

I encourage you to play around with these options. As always, your mileage may vary, but they are important tools to have in your toolset.

WORKING WITH A PHYSICAL DEVICE

When I have an actual Android device, in almost all cases I'll do development on it over the emulator. One of the wonderful things about Android is how utterly simple it is to connect and work with nearly any Android phone. Here's what you'll need to do if you want to start working with your own device.

1. Find the USB cable that came with your phone, and plug it into your computer.

2. For Android 2.x or 3.x, on your home screen, open your application drawer and look for the Settings app. From within the Settings app, choose Applications > Development. Select the USB Debugging check box.

   While you are in the application settings, also select the Unknown Sources check box.

   or

FIGURE 1.8 Enable USB debugging.　　　　　**FIGURE 1.9** Allow unknown sources.

For Android 4.0.x and above, on your home screen, open your application drawer and look for the Settings app. From within the Settings app, select Developer Options and toggle the Developer Options switch in the upper-right corner to On. Select the USB Debugging check box (**Figure 1.8**).

Then go to Settings > Security and select the Unknown Sources check box (**Figure 1.9**).

Enabling unknown sources lets you install applications that are not from Google Play onto your phone. It might be wise to disable this while you're not developing, to prevent any possibility of accidentally installing a non–Google Play application.

> **NOTE:** Starting in Android 4.2, the developer options on phones have been hidden by default. This is because there are many powerful options that can utterly destroy an application's performance, and most average users should not try to tinker with them. To find developer options on 4.2 and above, go to Settings > About Phone (or About Tablet). Look for the list item Build Number, and press it repeatedly until you start seeing toasts indicating you are only a few steps away from being a developer. When you see the message "You are now a developer," you can enable the developer options on the primary settings screen.

If you're on a Windows machine, you may need to install the general USB drivers. You can find them at http://developer.android.com/sdk/win-usb.html.

If you've finished everything correctly, you should see a little bug icon in the notification bar on your device. Your phone will work in exactly the same way an emulator would.

Congratulations! If you've followed every step thus far, you have your very own emulator or connected device, your Android SDK is correctly installed, and you're ready to rock and roll. Take a minute to play around with your new emulator before moving on to the next section, which is about creating applications.

> **TIP:** The emulator is a full Linux virtual machine and can be a little heavy on the system resources (especially while Eclipse is running), so make sure your development machine has plenty of RAM.

CREATING A NEW ANDROID PROJECT

FIGURE 1.10 Select the project type here.

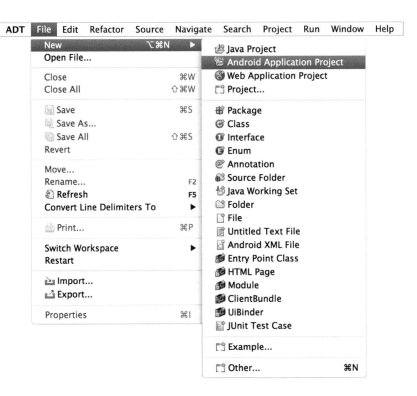

Creating a new project in Android has never been easier. Google has provided some very powerful tools that let you bootstrap a basic application in no time. We are going to use the basic project creation wizard to create our first application and learn how all these folders and source files interact with each other. Can't wait to get started? Me neither, so let's go!

1. In **Eclipse**, choose File > New > Android Application Project (**Figure 1.10**). If you don't see Android Application Project, select Other and search in the Android subfolder there.

   or

   In **Android Studio**, choose File > New Project.

2. Click Next, and Android's friendly project creation wizard starts. The project creation wizards for each IDE are styled differently, but they offer the same workflow and options (**Figures 1.11** and **1.12**).

   Let's go over what each field means to your project as you complete them. We're going to review the screenshots for Android Studio, but for the most part, the wizards are identical. If you don't see an option that's being described, it's most likely coming up on the next screen.

FIGURE 1.11 Enter all the pesky details for your Eclipse project here.

3. In the Application Name field, enter the full name of your application.

   This is what will show in the app drawer after you have installed your app.

4. Enter a project/module name. This name is how your IDE keeps track of your project. This name will never show up in your application or on the device, so it's OK to pick unique and descriptive names here.

5. Enter a package name. This is where all your Java source code is housed. It's common practice to have your package name mimic the name of its corresponding web service.

   For example, if you're making an application for purplepony.com, then you should probably name your package com.purplepony.

6. From the Target SDK menu, select the latest version of Android.

   Newer versions of Android always support applications built through older SDKs. They accomplish this with what's called *compatibility mode.* For now, try to target the most advanced version you can.

7. Leave the Compile With and Theme menus at their default values. As it suggests, this tells the compiler that you want to compile with the latest version of Android, and that you want to use the Light Holo theme with a dark action bar. We'll get more into themes later. Click Next.

> **NOTE:** Eclipse users: I'm not going to cover how to use the custom icon creator; it's self-explanatory. If you deselect it, a generic icon will be given to you. If you leave it selected, you will get to play around with some options on the next screen.

8. Leave the Create Activity check box selected, and leave the Mark This Project as a Library check box unselected.

   Library projects are powerful ways to share Android code between multiple projects. It's an advanced topic, so we're not going to get into it just yet.

9. Click Next through the remaining screens, and click Finish on the last screen. You are off to the races!

   Now that you have a project, let's get it running.

CREATING A PROJECT FROM THE COMMAND LINE FOR ECLIPSE

If you prefer to work from the command line, you can enter a few commands and move on with your day:

1. Enter android list targets on the command line, and press Enter. This will list the available targets on your system:

   id: 1 or "android-17"

   Name: Android 4.2.2

   Type: Platform

   API level: 17

   Revision: 2

   Skins: HVGA, QVGA, WQVGA400, WQVGA432, WSVGA, WVGA800 (default),
   → WVGA854, WXGA720, WXGA800, WXGA800-7in

   ABIs : armeabi-v7a

2. Enter the following commands, supplying the values for the highlighted items using the bullet list below as a guide:

   ```
   android create project -n MyFantasticSimpleProject -t 1 -p
   myProjectDirectory -k com.peachpit.fantasticProjctPackage -a
   NewActivity
   cd myProjectDirectory
   ant debug install
   ```

   - -n The name of your project

   - -t The build target for the project (corresponds to targets listed in first command)

   - -p The path to your project

   - -k The project's package name

   - -a The main activity

These commands create a new project and install a new application on an Android device. Assuming that you didn't run into any errors, you should find your sample app in the emulator's app drawer.

RUNNING YOUR NEW PROJECT

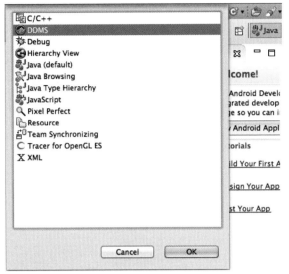

FIGURE 1.13 Select DDMS from the Open Perspective list.

FIGURE 1.14 If your device is recognized, it will appear in the devices list of your DDMS perspective.

Running your application is a satisfying experience. One of the great parts of the Android IDE is how it simplifies the build and execution process of your applications. As long as you can verify that your device is talking to the IDE properly (which we are about to cover), everything just sort of "works" and it's truly magical.

ECLIPSE

1. If your emulator isn't running, fire it up; if you're using a physical device, plug it into your computer's USB port.

2. To verify that Eclipse recognizes your emulator or device, you need to open the DDMS (Dalvik Debug Monitor Service) perspective: Choose Window > Open Perspective > Other, select DDMS from the list that appears, and click OK (**Figure 1.13**).

3. Verify that Eclipse recognizes your device by looking in the Devices tab of DDMS. If your device is connected, you will see it listed there by name, as well as all the processes that are currently running on it (**Figure 1.14**). If you don't see your device there, restart your emulator (or unplug your device) and try again. If you still don't see it, check out the end of this chapter for troubleshooting details.

4. Return to the Java perspective by clicking the Java tab, which is located next to the DDMS tab in the upper-right corner.

FIGURE 1.15 Connected devices in Android Studio show up in the Android DDMS tab, located in the lower-left corner of the application window.

5. From the Run menu, choose either "Run last launched" or Run. Eclipse may ask you to confirm that the app is indeed an Android project.

Android will compile, package, install, and run the application on your emulator or device. You've now officially created an Android application.

ANDROID STUDIO

1. At the bottom of the Android Studio window, click the Android tab (**Figure 1.15**). If your device has connected properly, you should see it here. If you don't see your device here, close your emulator or unplug your device. Wait a few seconds, and then turn it back on or plug it back in. If you still don't see it, check out the end of this chapter for troubleshooting details.

2. From the application window, choose Run > Run Your Application. A dialog will appear, asking which device you would like to run it on. Choose either your emulator or your device, and click OK. If all goes as planned, you should see your old friend "Hello world!" (**Figure 1.16** on the next page).

Although it doesn't do much, you've successfully created and run your first Android application. As Confucius said, a journey of a thousand miles begins with a single step.

> **TIP:** You can see all the Android device monitoring tools, including DDMS, by running `monitor` from the command line.

FIGURE 1.16 Your very first Android application, running on the emulator!

TROUBLESHOOTING THE EMULATOR

As a general rule, if things aren't working the way you expect them to, restart Eclipse. This isn't limited to Eclipse, of course; Android Studio will also need to be restarted from time to time. If ever you feel like something should "just work" and you've double-checked all your code, try restarting. I can't tell you how many times this has remedied a bug I'd thought I created. If restarting isn't doing it for you, here's a handy trick to try out.

If you're sure your emulator is running, but it refuses to display in the list of devices, you may need to restart the Android Debug Bridge (ADB). Doing this requires getting into the terminal a little bit.

1. If you haven't set up your command line path (bet you wish you did now), open a terminal window and change directories to the platform-tools folder inside your Android SDK folder.

   cd ~/Documents/adt_bundle/platform-tools.

2. Run adb kill-server and count to 15.

3. Run adb start-server.

   When you run the start command, you should see the following lines:

   * daemon not running. starting it now on port 5037 *

   * daemon started successfully *

4. Switch back to the DDMS perspective in Eclipse, or type **monitor**.

   You should see the virtual device listed in the devices window. If you don't, start from the beginning and restart the emulator, ADB, and your IDE until you do.

5. Switch back to the Java perspective and choose Run > Run.

6. When you're asked what kind of project it is, select Android.

   The dialog may ask which device you'd like to run your project on. Eclipse may also want to know which device you'd like to run your project on. Select emulator or device, depending on which option you're working with.

7. If you're using a physical device, now is the time to plug it in, or if using an emulator, this is your chance to start a new one. Otherwise, select one of the available devices and click OK.

WRAPPING UP

This chapter covered downloading, installing, configuring, creating, and running Android applications. You now have the basic tools that you'll need to continue with this book. Feel free, if you're struggling with the topics in later chapters, to refer back to this chapter as needed.

CHAPTER 2

Exploring the Application Basics

I'm sure you're ready to roll up your sleeves and write more code. However, there are a few topics in the realm of theory and design to cover in detail first. In this chapter, we'll cover the basics of some essential building blocks, including the files, parts, and terms that make up a simple Android application; the `Activity` class, which controls a single screen; the `Intent` class, Android's powerful communications class; and the `Application` singleton class, which can be accessed from all your components. There is one more key component for your Android toolset, the `Fragment`, but we'll cover that later on; it's not necessary to understanding the basics.

I recommend you open your IDE and follow along as I cover the working parts of an Android application. I'll be using the Android project that you created in Chapter 1.

THE FILES

Any mobile application, in its most basic form, consists of a single screen that is launched by clicking an icon on the device's main screen.

When the SDK creates a basic Android project, it also creates several files and important directories.

As with any project, before you start building the structure it's important to at least take a quick look over the blueprints. In an Android project, it is the files and folders that make up that structure.

In **Eclipse**, you will find your source folders and Android manifest right in the root directory:

- `AndroidManifest.xml`
- `/res`
- `/src`

    In **Android Studio**, you will find your source folders and Android manifest under

- `/projectName/src/main/AndroidManifest.xml`
- `/projectName/src/main/java`
- `/projectName/src/main/res`

Your application can have only one `AndroidManifest.xml` file, so I'll refer to this file and concept simply as the manifest.

THE MANIFEST

The `AndroidManifest.xml` file is your portal to the rest of the phone. In it, you'll describe which of your components should receive what events. You'll also declare, in the manifest file, what hardware and software your app will need permission to access. First, let's take a look at the `<manifest>` declaration in the `AndroidManifest.xml` file:

```
<manifest xmlns:android="http://schemas.android.com/apk/res/android"
    package="com.peachPit"
    android:versionCode="1"
    android:versionName="1.0">
```

There are a few noteworthy items in this code. The package definition tells Android which Java package to look in for the class files that make up the components of your application. The next two variables are not particularly important right now, but they will become vital once you're ready to ship your application to the Google Play Store. The `versionCode` is the number that helps Google Play alert users that an update is available. The `versionName` is a string that the application menus and Google Play display to the user as the current version of your app.

THE ACTIVITY CLASS

Open your manifest file, located in `<ProjectRoot>/AndroidManifest.xml` (If you don't open it in the IDE, make sure you open it with a text editor.) In a typical Android application, activities are the backbone of the operation. Essentially, their purpose is to control what is displayed on the screen. They bridge the gap between the data you wish to display and the UI layout files and classes that do the work of displaying the data. If you're familiar with the popular Model-View-Controller (MVC) architecture, the activity would be the control for a screen. Here's what the activity declaration looks like in the manifest file:

```
<activity android:name=".MainActivity"
   android:label="@string/app_name">
<!-- More on how the intent-filter works in the next section-->
   <intent-filter>
      <action android:name="android.intent.action.MAIN" />
      <category android:name="android.intent.category.LAUNCHER" />
   </intent-filter>
</activity>
```

The `android:name` tag tells the system what to place on the end of your package (from the manifest declaration) to find your class definition. For example, in my sample project at `com.peachpit.MainActivity`, the class loader looks for a class that extends the `Activity` class.

In order to be found, the file must reside under the `src/com/peachPit` directory. This is standard operating procedure for the language that Android uses.

WATCHING THE ACTIVITY IN ACTION

The activity, if used correctly, is an object that specifically controls a single screen.

Let's talk about this mythical activity in terms of a real-world RSS news feed reader—a case study that can quickly explain what pages of theory would often miss. A developer typically uses one activity to list all feeds to which a user has subscribed. When a user taps a feed, the developer uses a second activity to display a list of available articles for that particular news feed. Lastly, when a user clicks a particular story, the developer uses a third activity to display article details.

It's easy to see how activities fill a certain role (subscription list, article list, article detail). At the same time, the activities are general, in that the article list should be able to display a list of articles from any RSS feed, and the article-details activity should show the details from any article found through an RSS reader.

THE MOST BASIC OF ACTIVITIES

In its simplest form, an activity is an object that extends the `Activity` class. It only needs to implement the onCreate method and call setContentView to get a visible interface. Here's what your activity looks like by default when you create a new project:

```
public class MainActivity extends Activity {
    /** Called when the activity is first created. */
    @Override
    public void onCreate(Bundle savedInstanceState) {
        super.onCreate(savedInstanceState);
        setContentView(R.layout.main);
    }
}
```

In this code, the device calls the onCreate method as the activity is starting. onCreate tells the UI system that the setContentView method specifies the main layout file for this activity. Each activity can have one and only one content view, so once you set it, it can't be changed. This is how the Android SDK forces you to use a new activity for each screen, because each time you want to change your root content view, you'll need a different activity.

IMPLEMENTING YOUR OWN ACTIVITY

In most cases, the best way to understand something is to use it. With that in mind, let's add a new activity to the project you created in Chapter 1. This will explain how the activity works, its lifecycle, and what you need to know while working with it. Here are the general steps you'll need to follow.

1. Add an entry for the new activity to your manifest.
2. Create a new class that extends the Activity class.
3. Create a new file containing the XML layout instructions for this new activity, and add a new string literal for the layout to display (don't worry, this sounds a lot harder than it actually is).
4. When all the files are in place, you'll need to launch this new activity from your existing one.

TELLING ANDROID ABOUT YOUR NEW ACTIVITY

We need to add the activity declaration to the manifest so that the Android system knows where to find your new activity when it comes time to load and launch it.

1. Open the AndroidManifest.xml file in your IDE.
2. Add the following line inside the <application> tag and directly after the </activity> closing tag of the previous declaration:

   `<activity android:name=".NewActivity"/>`

   This little line tells the system where to find the new activity in your application package. In the case of my demo, the class loader knows to look for the activity at com.peachPit.NewActivity.

   Next, you'll need to put a file there for it to find.

CREATING THE NEWACTIVITY CLASS

There are several ways to create a new activity, but here is the easiest way to do it in your IDE.

1. Right-click (or Control-click) the package name you've chosen (mine is `com.peachPit`).

2. Select New, then select Class.

3. Name your new class **NewActivity**.

4. In the Superclass field, click the browse button.

5. In the Superclass window search field, start typing **Activity** until you see Activity–android.app populate. When you see it, select it, and click OK.

   Although a name is technically all you need to create a new class, adding the superclass from this window will ensure that you are always extending the class you intended. This can really be a lifesaver when you start dealing with compatibility components that have the same name across different libraries.

6. Make the following highlighted changes to your code:

```
package com.peachPit;

import android.app.Activity;

import android.os.Bundle;

public class NewActivity extends Activity{


    @Override public void onCreate(Bundle savedInstanceState){

        super.onCreate(savedInstanceState);

    }

}
```

   Notice that this code looks very similar to what is already in your existing activity. Let's make it a little bit different. If the imports don't automatically appear for you, choose Source > Organize Imports. This will make sure you have all the imports you need included, as well as remove any unused ones.

7. In the `res/values/strings.xml` file, add the following highlighted lines in the `<resources>` tag under the existing strings:

```
<resources>

    <!–other strings are omitted here for brevity-->

    <string name="new_activity_text">

        Welcome to the New Activity!

    </string>

</resources>
```

> **NOTE:** `"new_activity_text"` is just a variable name. You can name it whatever makes the most sense for you and your project.

There are a few ways to edit XML in your IDE, and there is no single right answer

- **Android common XML editor (the visual editor).** This editor is a great way to quickly add strings on the fly. This is the editor that the IDE will open by default if you don't change it. It will always have at least two tabs at the bottom of the window. The last of those tabs shows the raw source XML, in which you can manually type (with auto-complete of course). The first tabs show a visual editor for managing the resource's contents. Whether you're configuring the manifest or adding a new string, it's a great way to visualize what components are available to you to customize.

- **IDE XML editor.** The classic way of editing XML files. If you come from a long background in Eclipse or Intellij, then this stock editor might be more comfortable for you, but I wouldn't recommend it. The auto-completion capabilities in the common editor far surpass the ones available here.

- **Text editor.** Once you have Android XML completely memorized, you might consider using a plain text editor. Although you won't get auto-complete, you won't be fighting the system over layout files that you know are not broken.

In these lines, you told Android that you want a new string with the name new_activity_ text that can be accessed through Android's resource manager. You'll learn much more about the contents of the /values folder in later chapters. Next, you need to create a layout file for your new activity.

CREATING A NEW SCREEN LAYOUT

Here's how you create a new layout.

1. Create a file named `activity_new.xml` inside the `res/layout/` folder. It should sit next to the existing `main.xml` file (which is used by your existing activity). This `activity_new.xml` file should look almost exactly like `main.xml`, except you'll need to add a reference to the string you just created.

2. Inside `activity_new.xml`, insert the following code to create a basic layout with a text view in it. By adding `android:id="@+id/new_activity_text_view"`, you are assigning this TextView an ID so your Java code can reference it (you'll learn more about TextViews later; for now you should know that they're Android views that show text on the screen):

```xml
<?xml version="1.0" encoding="utf-8"?>

<LinearLayout xmlns:android="http://schemas.android.com/apk/res/android"
    android:orientation="vertical"
    android:layout_width="match_parent"
    android:layout_height="match_parent" >
<TextView
        android:id="@+id/new_activity_text_view"
```

```
        android:layout_width="match_parent"
      android:layout_height="wrap_content"
      android:text="@string/new_activity_text" />


  </LinearLayout>
```

I devote Chapter 3 to resource management and user interface design, but for now just keep in mind that the @ prefix is how you tell Android that you want to reference an ID, string, or drawable that is defined elsewhere as a resource.

Now that you have a new layout with a shiny new string, you'll need to tell the NewActivity class that you want it to use this particular layout file.

3. Add the following highlighted line to the onCreate method of your NewActivity class:

```
public void onCreate(Bundle icicle){
    super.onCreate(icicle);
    setContentView(R.layout.activity_new);
}
```

setContentView is the method in which you tell Android which XML file to display for your new activity. Now that you've created a new class, string, and layout file, it's time to launch the activity and display your new view on the screen.

PUSHING THE BUTTON

The simplest way to launch your new activity on a device is to touch it. Launching an activity just by touching the screen probably isn't a very common use case in practice, but it makes for a good and simple example. Most new activities are started when a user selects a list item, presses a button, or takes another action with the screen.

Inside your MainActivity (the one that was auto-generated for you when you made the project), add the following code :

```
public class MainActivity extends Activity {
    public void onCreate(Bundle icicle){
        super.onCreate(icicle);
        setContentView(R.layout.activity_new);

        View view = getWindow().getDecorView()
            .findViewById(android.R.id.content);
        view.setOnClickListener(new OnClickListener() {
            @Override
            public void onClick(View v) {
                // Launch new Activity here!
            }
        });
    }
}
```

Important: After you add this code, in **Eclipse** choose Source > Organize Imports; in **Android Studio**, choose Code > Optimize Imports. If your IDE is confused about which OnClickListener to import, select View.OnClickListener (not Dialog.OnClickListener). Organizing your imports is something that you will need to do on a fairly regular basis while building applications, so this one might be worth learning the shortcuts for. Check out the Source menu in Eclipse or the Code menu in Android studio; the keyboard shortcuts will be listed next to the name.

By setting an OnClickListener on the view, you are letting the system know that you want a callback if this view is clicked. Don't worry about the getWindow() and getDecorView() functions for now; they are just a quick way of catching clicks on the entire screen. Later on I'll show you how to set these click listeners on actual buttons and other views.

LAUNCHING THE ACTIVITY

Finally, it's time to launch the new activity. This will start your brief foray into intents. Each new activity is started as the result of a new intent being dispatched into the system (which processes it and takes the appropriate action). To start the first activity, you'll need a reference of your application context and the class object for your new activity. Let's create the new intent first.

1. Place the following code into your onClick method:

```
Intent startIntent=new Intent(MainActivity.this,
    NewActivity.class);
```

You will probably need to organize your imports after adding the Intent. You're passing the new intent a context (MainActivity.this is an easy way to reference the parent activity, which itself is a subclass of Context) and the class object of the activity that you would like to launch. This tells Android exactly where to look in the application package. There are many ways to create and interact with intents; this is, however, the simplest way to start up a new activity.

2. Once the intent is properly constructed, it's simply a matter of telling the Android system that you'd like to start the new activity. Put the following line into your onClick method after the intent:

```
startActivity(startIntent);
```

Your OnClickListener should now look like the following:

```
View view = getWindow().getDecorView()
    .findViewById(android.R.id.content);
view.setOnClickListener(new OnClickListener() {
  @Override
  public void onClick(View v) {
      Intent startIntent = new Intent(MainActivity.this, NewActivity.class)
      startActivity(startIntent);
  }
});
```

FIGURE 2.1 Here is your new activity!

NOTE: Throughout this whole process, the original activity has never once had access to the instance of the new activity. Any information that might pass between these two activities must go through the intermediary intent. You'll learn how this is done in the section "The Intent Class."

TRYING IT OUT

If you're running your IDE and you've been coding along with me, it should now be a simple matter of spinning up the emulator and installing your new activity (the steps for which you should remember from Chapter 1). Once your new application has launched, press the center key to see the results of your labor (**Figure 2.1**).

Now that you know how to create and launch a new activity, it's time to discuss how that process works. You'll need to understand, for the purposes of UI layout and data management/retention later, what methods are called each time one of your activities makes its way onto, and off of, the screen.

In the source documentation on intents, they are described as "An abstract description of an operation to be performed." Intents can take a myriad of forms, but really they're just a plain Java object that tells the system that you intend to do something. *Intend* is the key word here, since the system is the thing that actually takes what you intend to do and figures out how to handle it. This leave all the messy launching of new activities and sharing information between other applications up to the system instead of you.

You use them anytime you need to start an activity or service. Further, you'll frequently use intents for system-wide communication. For example, you can receive notifications about power system changes by registering for a widely published intent. If one of your activities registers for an intent in the manifest (for example, com.peachPit.OhOhPickMe), then any application anywhere on the phone can; if you make your activity public, launch directly to your activity by calling

```
startActivity(new Intent("com.peachpit.OhOhPickMe"));
```

THE LIFE AND TIMES OF AN ACTIVITY

Each activity lives a very short but exciting life. It begins when an intent that your activity is registered to receive is broadcast to the system. The system calls your activity's constructor (while also starting your application as necessary) before invoking the following methods on the activity, in this order:

- onCreate
- onStart
- onResume

When you implement an activity, it's your job to extend the methods that make up this lifecycle. The only one you are required to extend is onCreate. The others, if you declare them, will be called in the lifecycle order.

Your activity is the top visible application, can draw to the screen, will receive key events, and is generally the life of the party. When the user presses the Back key from the activity, these corresponding methods are called in the following order:

- onPause
- onStop
- onDestroy

After these methods have executed, your activity is closed down and should be ready for garbage collection.

THE SHORT, BRUTAL LIFE OF THE ACTIVITY

An activity's life is incredibly short. They are constantly created and destroyed, so it's very important that you save no data in them that has any relevance outside the screen your activity will control.

The following are all valid actions that will result in the destruction of any activity:

- The user rotated the device from portrait to landscape or vice versa.

- The activity is no longer visible onscreen or the system is low on resources.

- It's Tuesday.

- The user has pressed the Back or Home button and left your application.

Again, make sure the data members of your activity pertain only to the elements on the screen. Further, don't expect the activity to save any data for you. You'll learn strategies to handle this in later chapters.

In order to make sense of the activity's flow, let's quickly look over each lifecycle method in detail. Remember that you must evoke the superclass call in each of these methods (often before you do anything else) or Android will throw exceptions at you.

> **NOTE:** onCreate is the only one of the application lifecycle methods that you must implement. I usually end up implementing only one or two of these methods, depending on what each activity is responsible for.

PUBLIC VOID ONCREATE(BUNDLE SAVEDINSTANCESTATE)

Android will call your declaration of the onCreate method as your activity is starting, and it will be called only once per activity lifecycle. Remember that if the user rotates the device, the activity will be destroyed and re-created, at which point onCreate would be called again, but that's because it's a new activity.

The onCreate method is the place to do things you want to do only once. For example, if the title for your activity is dynamic but will not change after the activity is started, onCreate would be where you'd want to reach into the view hierarchy and set up the title. This method is not the place to configure data that could change while the app is in the background or when another activity is launched on top of it—that we're saving for onResume.

Further, if your app is running in the background and the system is running low on resources, your application may be killed. If that happens, the onCreate method will be called on a new instance of the same activity when your application returns to the foreground.

The onCreate method is also your one and only chance to call setContentView for your activity. This, as you saw earlier, is how you tell the system what layout you'd like to use for this screen. You call setContentView once you can begin setting data on the UI. This could be anything from setting the contents of lists to TextViews or ImageViews.

PUBLIC VOID ONSTART( )

When starting up, your onStart method is called immediately after onCreate. If your app was put in the background (either by another application launching over yours or because the user pressed the Home button), onStart will be called as you resume but before the activity can interact with the screen. I tend to avoid overriding onStart unless there's something specific I need to check when my application is about to begin using the screen.

PUBLIC VOID ONRESUME( )

onResume is the last method called in the activity lifecycle as your activity is allowed access to the screen. If UI elements changed while your activity was in the background, this method is the place to make sure the UI and phone state are in sync.

When your activity is starting up, this method is called after onCreate and onStart. When your activity is coming to the foreground again, regardless of what state it was in before, onResume will always be called. This is a great place to make network calls to make sure that data is refreshed every time you come back to this activity.

HOORAY, YOUR ACTIVITY IS NOW RUNNING!

After all this setup, configuration, and work, your activity is now visible to the user. Things are being clicked, data may be parsed and displayed, lists are scrolled, and things are happening! At some point, however, the party must end (perhaps because the user pressed the Back key), and you'll need to wind things down.

ONPAUSE( )

onPause is the first method called by the system as your application is leaving the screen. If you have any processes or loops (animations, for example) that should be running only while your activity is onscreen, the onPause method is the perfect place to stop them. onPause will be called on your activity if you've launched another activity over the one you're currently displaying.

Keep in mind that if the system needs resources, your process could be killed anytime after the onPause method is called. This isn't a normal occurrence, but you need to be aware that it could happen.

The onPause method is important because it may be the only warning you get that your activity (or even your entire application) is going away. It is in this method that you should save any important information to disk, your database, or the preferences.

Once your activity has actually left the screen, you'll receive the next call in the activity lifecycle.

ONSTOP( )

When Android calls your onStop method, it indicates that your activity has officially left the screen. Further, onStop is called when the user is leaving your activity to interact with another one. This doesn't necessarily mean that your activity is shutting down (although it could). You can only assume that the user has left your activity for another one. If you're doing any ongoing processing from within your activity that should run only while it's active, this method is your chance to be a good citizen and shut it down.

ONDESTROY( )

onDestroy is your last method call before oblivion. This is your last chance for your activity to clean up its affairs before it passes on to the great garbage collector in the sky.

Any background processes that your activity may have been running in the background (fetching/parsing data, for example) must be shut down on this method call.

However, just because onDestroy is called doesn't mean that your activity will be obliterated; it just marks the application as ready to be cleaned up so that whenever the garbage collector requires more resources, it knows that it is allowed to garbage-collect this application. So if you have a thread running and downloading data in the background, it may continue to run and take up system resources even after the onDestroy method is called unless you explicitly cancel it here.

BONUS ROUND—DATA RETENTION METHODS

As mentioned, your process can be killed at any point after onPause if the system needs resources. The user, however, shouldn't ever know that this culling has occurred. Android gives you two chances to save your state data for later use.

ONSAVEINSTANCESTATE(BUNDLE OUTSTATE)

This method passes you a bundle object into which you can put any data that you'd need to restore your activity to its current state at a later time. You'll do this by calling something like outState.putString(...) or outState.putBoolean(...). Each stored value requires a string key going in, and it requires the same string key to come back out. You are responsible for overriding your own onSaveInstanceState method. If you've declared it, the system will call it; otherwise, you've missed your chance.

When your previously killed activity is restored, the system will call your onCreate method again and hand back to you the bundle you built with onSaveInstanceState.

onSaveInstanceState will be called only if the system thinks you may have to restore your activity later—for instance, if you received a phone call. It wouldn't be called if, for example, the user has pressed the Back key, as the device clearly has no need to resume this exact activity later. As such, this method is not the place for saving user data. Only stash temporary information that is important to the UI on this particular instance of the screen.

ONRETAINNONCONFIGURATIONINSTANCE( )

When the user switches between portrait and landscape mode, your activity is destroyed and a new instance of it is created (going through the full shutdown-startup cycle of method calls). When your activity is destroyed and created specifically because of a configuration change (the device rotation being the most common), onRetainNonConfigurationInstance gives you a chance to return any object that can be reclaimed in your new activity instance by calling getLastNonConfigurationInstance. This is great for saving large amounts of data, like images or big network requests, that you wouldn't normally be able to serialize into the outState from onSaveInstanceState.

This tactic helps make screen rotation transitions faster. Keep this in mind if it takes your activity a significant amount of time to acquire data that it plans to display on the screen. Instead, you can get the previously displayed data by using getLastNonConfigurationInstance.

Here's an example of how to use onRetainNonConfigurationInstance:

```
@Override
public Object onRetainNonConfigurationInstance() {
    final DataModel data = getFetchedData();
    return data;
}
@Override
public void onCreate(Bundle savedInstanceState) {
    super.onCreate(savedInstanceState);
    setContentView(R.layout.main);

    DataModel data = (DataModel) getLastNonConfigurationInstance();
    if (data == null) {
        data = fetchData();
    }
}
```

You should now have a basic understanding of

- Steps for creating a new activity
- How an activity is started
- The lifecycle of an activity

You have what you need to keep up as I go over more complex topics in later chapters. Fear not, I'll come back to the activity in no time.

THE INTENT CLASS

Intents, in the Android platform, make up the major communication protocol for moving information between application components. In a well-designed Android application, components (activity, content provider, or service) should never directly access an instance of any other component. As such, intents are how these pieces are able to communicate.

A good half of this book could be dedicated to the creation, use, and details of the Intent class. For the sake of brevity and getting you up and running as fast as possible, I'll cover only a few basics in this chapter. Look for intents throughout the rest of this book. They're probably the most-used class in Android as a whole.

There are two main ways to tell the Android system that you'd like to receive intents sent out by the system, by other applications, or even by your own app:

- Registering an `<intent-filter>` in the `AndroidManifest.xml` file
- Registering an `IntentFilter` object at runtime with the system

In each case, you need to tell the Android system what events you want to listen for.

There are numerous ways of sending intents as well. You can broadcast them out to the system as a whole, or you can target them to a specific activity or service. However, to start a service or activity, it must be registered in the manifest (you saw an example of this in the previous demonstration on starting a new activity).

Let's take a look at how to use intents in practice.

MANIFEST REGISTRATION

Why not register everything at runtime? If an intent is declared as part of your manifest, the system will start your component so that it will receive it. Registration at runtime presupposes that you are already running. For this reason, anytime you want your application to awaken and take action based on an event, declare it in your manifest. If it's something your application should receive only while it's running, register an `IntentFilter` (it's an `intent-filter` when declared in XML, but an `IntentFilter` in your Java code) once your particular component has started.

Let's go back to the initial application and look again at the activity's entry in the manifest:

```
<activity android:name=".MainActivity"
    android:label="@string/app_name">
    <intent-filter>
        <action android:name="android.intent.action.MAIN" />
        <category android:name="android.intent.category.LAUNCHER" />
    </intent-filter>
</activity>
```

The `android.intent.action.MAIN` declaration tells the system that this activity is the main activity for your application. No parameters are needed to start it. It's a good idea to list only one activity as MAIN in the manifest. This is also how ADB (the Android Debug Bridge) knows which activity to start up.

The android.intent.category.LAUNCHER category tells the system that the enclosing activity should be launched when your icon is clicked on the phone's application dock. Further, it tells Android that you'd like the icon to appear in the app launcher drawer. This is an example of an intent-filter that's created for you by Android's project creation tools. Let's add one of our own.

ADDING AN INTENT

If you skipped the previous section about the Activity class, now may be a good time to go back and at least skim over the code. In that section, I showed you how to declare and launch a simple new activity. What I didn't show you, however, was how to make that activity accessible to the system as a whole by declaring an <intent-filter> for it within your manifest. Let's do that now.

1. Add an intent-filter to the NewActivity declaration:

```
<activity android:name=".NewActivity">

  <intent-filter>

    <action android:name="com.peachpit.PURPLE_PONY_POWER"/>

    <category android:name="android.intent.category.DEFAULT"/>

  </intent-filter>

</activity>
```

In this code, you've registered for intents containing the com.peachpit.PURPLE_PONY_ POWER action and set the intent-filter category to default.

Now, lest you think I'm a crazed children's toy enthusiast, I've used this rather absurdist action string to demonstrate a point—namely, that the only requirement for the action string is that it be unique for your particular component.

In the previous section, I showed you how to launch the new activity by using the following lines:

```
Intent startIntent = new Intent(MainActivity.this, NewActivity.class);
startActivity(startIntent);
```

This works, but it has one major limitation: It cannot be launched outside your own application's context. This renders useless one of the most powerful features that the activity-intent model has to offer. Namely, any application on the device, with the right intent, can use components within your application.

Now that you've added the <intent-filter> to the sample project manifest, you can launch this particular activity anywhere with the following code:

```
Intent actionStartIntent = new Intent("com.peachpit.PURPLE_PONY_POWER");
startActivity(actionStartIntent);
```

Notice a very important difference between this code and the listing above it. When you create the intent in this example, you're not required to pass in a Context object (the bundle of information that is required to communicate with the system at large). This allows any application, with knowledge of the required intents, to start the NewActivity class.

2. In your OnClickListener, replace your previous intent code with this new action intent code that's highlighted below. It should look like this:

```
view.setOnClickListener(new OnClickListener() {
@Override
   public void onClick(View v) {
      Intent actionStartIntent = new Intent("com.peachpit.
PURPLE_PONY_POWER");
      startActivity(actionStartIntent);
   }
});
```

Now when you press the down key in the sample application, you'll see the same activity launching using this new manifest-declared intent-filter.

If you've misspelled the intent's action string or neglected to add the default category to your intent-filter, you may get an android.content.Activity NotFoundException.

This exception will be thrown by the startActivity method anytime you create an intent that the system cannot connect to an activity listed in a manifest on the device.

Registering for intent filters is not only the purview of the activity. Any Android application component can register to be started when an intent action is broadcast by the system.

LISTENING FOR INTENTS AT RUNTIME

Another method for receiving events that pertain only to your application or for receiving events broadcast by the Android system itself is to listen for the intents at runtime.

Let's say that your activity would like to show a special screen or take a custom action when the user enables Airplane mode. To do this, you'll need to create a temporary IntentFilter and an inner BroadcastReceiver object instance.

CREATE A RECEIVER

Let's add the runtime BroadcastReceiver to the MainActivity class. A BroadcastReceiver is, as you can probably guess, an object with a single onReceive method. Remember to organize your imports after adding the BroadcastReceiver to make sure the class is recognized.

Change the MainActivity class to look like the following:

```
public class MainActivity extends Activity {
    private BroadcastReceiver simpleReceiver=new BroadcastReceiver() {
        public void onReceive(Context context, Intent intent) {
            if(intent.getAction().equals(
                Intent.ACTION_AIRPLANE_MODE_CHANGED)){
                    Toast.makeText(context,
                    R.string.airplane_change,
                    Toast.LENGTH_LONG).show();
            }
        }
    };
//Rest of the Activity is here.
}
```

In this code, you are creating a locally accessible receiver for use within the activity. When the system calls onReceive, you'll need to check what the intent's action is. This is a good idea, as BroadcastReceiver could register for any number of different intents.

When you receive the event that you're looking for, you'll use Android's Toast API to print a simple message on the screen (in this case, the contents of the string named airplane_change). In practice, this might be the time to show a screen indicating that network connectivity is required for the application to run correctly.

TELL ANDROID WHAT YOU WANT TO HEAR

Now that you've created a BroadcastReceiver, you can register it with the system:

```
public void onCreate(Bundle savedInstanceState) {
    super.onCreate(savedInstanceState);
    setContentView(R.layout.main);
    IntentFilter intentFilter = new IntentFilter();
    intentFilter.addAction(Intent.ACTION_AIRPLANE_MODE_CHANGED);
    registerReceiver(simpleReceiver, intentFilter);
}
```

This is going to be the primary way that your applications listen for information on the status of the system. Everything from the status of the battery to the status of the Wi-Fi radio is at your fingertips with this tool. You can find out more about what activities you can monitor, with what permissions, by looking in the Android SDK documentation for the Intent class.

CREATING SELF-CONTAINED BROADCAST RECEIVERS

A BroadcastReceiver doesn't have to exist inside an activity. You can register a receiver if you want to know about a system event but might not need to start your full application when it occurs.

BroadcastReceivers can be registered on their own under the <receiver> tag. In practice, I use these as a way to receive information about the system that may not require showing something to the user. Starting an activity only to shut it down if it's not needed is much more resource expensive than grabbing the broadcast intent with a receiver and then starting up an activity only when needed.

REMEMBER TO STOP LISTENING

For every runtime registration that you create, you must also unregister it. If you would like to receive the events only when your activity is visible, onPause is the best place to turn off the receiver. If you'd like to listen for as long as your activity is running, even if it's not visible, you'll want to unregister in onDestroy. Wherever you decide to stop listening, simply call unregisterReceiver (a method implemented by your superclass) and pass in the BroadcastReceiver you created earlier, like this:

```
@Override
public void onDestroy(){
    super.onDestroy();
    unregisterReceiver(simpleReceiver);
}
```

WRAPPING UP THE FLIGHT MODE RECEIVER

Again, this is all in the original MainActivity class made by the SDK when you created the project.

1. In the onCreate method, create an intent filter and add the action Intent.ACTION_ AIRPLANE_MODE_CHANGED to it.

2. Add as many actions to this intent filter as you wish. When your receiver is called, you'll have to sort out which intent actually triggered the onReceive method for the BroadcastReceiver by calling getAction() on the intent.

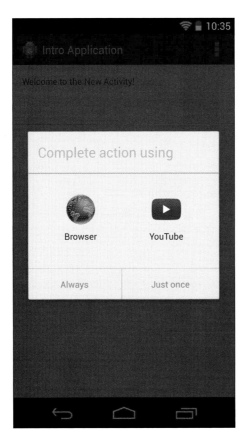

3. Test the code by holding the power button down; this will pop up a dialog with several options.

4. Enable Airplane mode. If you've done everything right so far, you should see a small message pop up along the bottom of the screen with your alert message in it.

5. Clean up by unregistering the BroadcastReceiver in onDestroy.

HANDLING COLLIDING ACTIVITIES

You may be thinking to yourself "Self, what happens when more than one activity is registered for the same intent?" This is a very interesting question, one that Android resolves simply by asking the user.

If two activities listen for the same intent in their manifests, and an application attempts to start an activity with that intent, the system will pop up a menu giving users a list of possible applications to choose from (**Figure 2.2**).

You've probably seen similar behavior hundreds of times on your desktop computer, such as when opening a file and being given a choice about which application you'd like to open it with.

This notion of many activities registering for the same intent can have delightful side effects. In Android, any application can register to share media with a given MIME time by using the `android.intent.action.SEND` action.

Figure 2.3 is what the Share tab on my phone looks like when I press it in the image gallery.

It is this ability to register for similar intents that allows seamless interaction, as each application registering this intent is given an entry on the Share menu. Clicking an entry in this list will start the registered activity and pass along as an extra the location at which the image can be accessed. What is an extra? Good question.

MOVING YOUR OWN DATA

One of the major features of the intent is the ability to package and send data along with it. One activity should never directly manipulate the memory of another. However, they still must have a way to communicate information. This communication is accomplished with the help of the intent's `Extra` bundle. The bundle can hold any number of string-primitive pairs. Perhaps the best way to illustrate this concept is with some code and an example.

Earlier, I showed you how to start a new activity by using an action-based broadcast intent.

Add the following highlighted code to the `OnClickListener` that you've dealt with before:

```
view.setOnClickListener(new OnClickListener() {
   @Override
   public void onClick(View v) {
      Intent actionStartIntent = new
         Intent("com.peachpit.PURPLE_PONY_POWER");
      actionStartIntent.putExtra("newBodyText",
         "You touched the screen!");
      startActivity(actionStartIntent);
   }
});
```

You're adding a string payload to the intent before using it to start an activity. Whoever receives the intent will be able to pull this string out (assuming they know it's there) and use it as they see fit. Now that you know how to attach the data, let's take a look at an example of retrieving and using the string in NewActivity's onCreate method:

```
public void onCreate(Bundle icicle){
   super.onCreate(icicle);
   setContentView(R.layout. activity_new);
   Intent currentIntent = getIntent();
   if(currentIntent.hasExtra("newBodyText")){
      String newText = currentIntent.getExtras().
         getString("newBodyText");
      TextView bodyView = (TextView)findViewById(
         R.id.new_activity_text_view);
      bodyView.setText(newText);
   }
```

In the highlighted code, I'm getting the intent that was responsible for starting my NewActivity by calling getIntent. Next, I'm checking if this intent actually contains the newBodyText extra. Keep in mind that the intent may not contain the extra. If you forget to check for this case, you'll quickly find yourself inundated with `NullPointerExceptions`. If the extra is there, I'll pull it out and set the string as the new text in my display. The last two lines obtain a reference to the screen's text view and change the text to be the contents of the extra. Don't worry about the mechanics of that particular operation right now; you'll learn about this topic in depth later.

REVIEWING INTENTS

You've learned how to register for, create, and use the basic functionality of an intent. As you now know, they can be registered for in the manifest or at runtime. They can be sent by any application on the phone, and any number of application components can register for the same intent.

The goal in this section was to get you started on the care and feeding of Android intents. In future chapters and tasks, you'll work with intents again in many different contexts.

THE APPLICATION CLASS

Typically, an Android application is a collection of activities, broadcast receivers, services, and content providers. The Application class is the glue that binds all these disparate pieces into a singular, unified entity. Every time a content provider, activity, service, or intent receiver in your manifest is initialized, an Application class is also spun up and available to it.

THE DEFAULT APPLICATION DECLARATION

Looking in the AndroidManifest.xml file, you'll see a typical Application declaration that looks like the following:

```
<application android:icon="@drawable/icon"
   android:label="@string/app_name">
<!-Activities, Services, Broadcast Receivers, and Content Providers -->
</application>
```

Here you can see the <application> tag. This part of the manifest typically contains information relevant to your application at large. android:icon tells the system what icon to display in the main application list. android:label in this case refers to another entry in the strings.xml file you were editing earlier.

CUSTOMIZING YOUR OWN APPLICATION

Adding your own application is very similar to the steps you've already gone through to add a new activity.

1. Add a name field to the existing AndroidManifest.xml declaration.
2. Create a new class in your package that extends the Application class.
3. Profit!

Let's go over steps 1 and 2 in depth. You're on your own for step 3.

THE NAME

When it comes to the manifest, android:name refers not to the name of the object being described, but to the location of the class in your Java package. The Application declaration is no exception. Here's what the opening tag of the application should look like with the new declaration:

```
<application android:icon="@drawable/icon"
   android:label="@string/app_name"
   android:name= ".SampleApplication">
```

In this declaration, you tell the system what icon you want to represent your application on the Android application drawer.

Once again, the class loader will look for your `Application` class by appending the contents of `android:name` to the end of your package declaration within the `<manifest>` opening tag. Now you'll need to actually create this class to keep the class loader from getting unhappy.

THE APPLICATION CLASS

Here's what you'll need, at a very basic level, to have an `Application` of your very own:

```
import android.app.Application;
public class SampleApplication extends Application{
    public void onCreate(){
        super.onCreate();
    }
}
```

The `Application` can be a very simple class. It's hard to understand what the `Application` can do for you until you consider a few things:

- Activities are very transient.
- Activities have no access to each other's memory, and they should communicate through intents.
- Because activities are constantly being stopped and started for a variety of reasons, there's no way for your activity to know if it's being started for the very first time in the run of your application. The `Application` class's onCreate method, on the other hand, is called only when your app is being initialized. As such, it can be a good place to take actions that should happen only when your application is first started.

If you need a temporary holding pen for data that may span many activities, a data member that's part of the `Application` can be a convenient place to store it. You must be very careful about adding data to the `Application`. Any single component declared in your manifest, from the simplest `BroadcastReceiver` to the most complex activity, will, before it's created by the system, first create your `Application` object. This means you must make the `Application`'s onCreate method run as fast as you possibly can.

ACCESSING THE APPLICATION

All your broadcast receivers, services, activities, and content providers have a method named getApplication provided to them by the appropriate superclass. When invoked, getApplication will return a reference to your `Application` object if you specified one in the manifest. Getting access to it, now that you've declared and created the class, is as simple as calling getApplication and casting the returned object to an instance of your own reference. Here's what it looks like:

```
SampleApplication myApplication = (SampleApplication) getApplication();
```

That's all there is to it. You can add public data members or context-sensitive methods to your own version of the Application, and with one call all your components have access to the same object, like so:

```java
public class SampleApplication extends Application{
   public String username;
   public void onCreate(){
      super.onCreate();
   }
}
```

To access your newly added variable, simply do the object cast listed earlier:

```java
public void onCreate(Bundle bundle){
   SampleApplication myApplication =
      (SampleApplication) getApplication();
   myApplication.username = "sparks";
}
```

Be sure that any data you put in the Application is relevant everywhere, because the overhead for allocating and initializing the Application can become a drag on startup times.

WRAPPING UP

Over the course of this chapter, I've exposed you to the fundamental building blocks of an Android application. I used examples to get you started on

- The manifest
- Creating and using your own activities
- Sending, receiving, and taking advantage of intents
- Creating your own Application object

It's my hope that through the rest of the book, you'll be able to use the building blocks you've learned in this chapter to understand how an Android application functions. From here on out, I'll be focusing more on how to do tasks rather than on the theories that back them. On that note, let's start making screens that include more than just a single text view.

CHAPTER 3

Creating User Interfaces

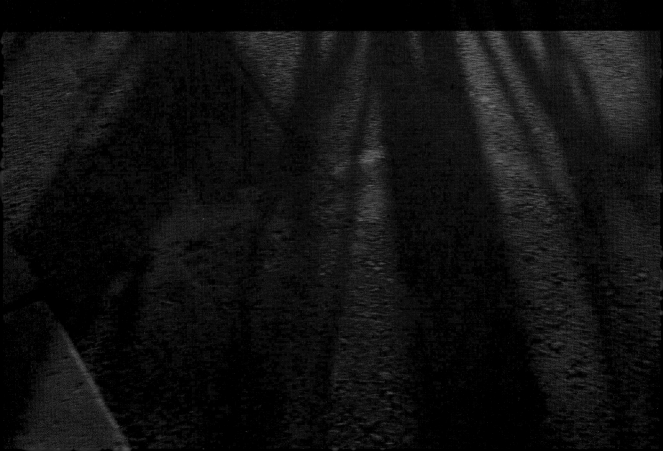

Creating an intuitive, good-looking interface is one of the most important aspects of a successful Android application. It doesn't matter how wonderful your code is if the user cannot easily find and use the features you've worked so hard to create. Although Android's diversity may give your application access to a greater pool of devices, you must also contend with making sure your application correctly supports multiple screen sizes.

Fortunately, Android gives developers many tools to make the process as straightforward as possible. In this chapter, you'll learn about all but one of the major building blocks for displaying information. The one major omission is the `ListView` class, which will be covered in a chapter of its own because it has a few unique concepts that don't apply to a standard view.

THE VIEW CLASS

No, this isn't a television show where several women debate the merits of common culture. The View class is the superclass for all the Android display objects. Each and every user interface (UI) class—from the simple ImageView to the mighty RelativeLayout—subclasses from this same object. In this section, you'll learn the basics of creating, adding, and modifying your existing layouts using Java code and XML. You'll also learn to create your own custom view. A view, at its very core, is simply a rectangle into which you can display something. Subclasses take many different forms, but they all serve the same purpose: to show something to the user.

CREATING A VIEW

Creating a new view is something you've already done. In Chapter 1, you added a view to an XML layout file as part of exploring how to launch a new activity. At the time, I told you we'd get into the specifics of how these views were created and modified, and, well, now's the time! Let's take a look at the default views generated for you automatically when you create a new Android project.

VIEWS IN XML

Here's what the default XML layout looks like in a new project:

```xml
<?xml version="1.0" encoding="utf-8"?>
<LinearLayout xmlns:android="http://schemas.android.com/apk/res/
    android"
    android:orientation="vertical"
    android:layout_width="match_parent"
    android:layout_height="match_parent" >
<TextView
    android:layout_width="match_parent"
    android:layout_height="wrap_content"
    android:text="@string/hello" />
</LinearLayout>
```

Question: Which of the two elements (LinearLayout and TextView) in this default XML layout is a view?

Answer: Both.

All visual objects onscreen subclass from the View class. If you go high enough in the inheritance chain, you'll find an "extends View" somewhere.

In the default XML layout, the Android tools have added a simple TextView contained inside a LinearLayout. When displayed onscreen, the contents of the hello string will appear by default in the upper-left corner of the screen. I'll discuss how to position visual elements onscreen later in this chapter.

For now, it's important to note that every single layout *must* have a value set for both its height and its width. Android may not fail to compile if you do not specify these values (as they could be updated at runtime), but if it starts to draw your views and the system height and width values are missing, then your application will crash.

To display the XML layout onscreen, you need to call the setContentView() method and pass the name of the layout to the activity.

From the code editor in your IDE, you should be able to find code in your activity that looks like this:

```
@Override
public void onCreate(Bundle savedInstanceState) {
    super.onCreate(savedInstanceState);
    setContentView(R.layout.main);
}
```

In this code, you're telling the activity that you want it to inflate and render the main layout for this activity. By inflating, I mean the conversion from the XML in the project to a Java object that can be told to draw on the screen. You might be thinking, "Is it possible to build and display a layout and view within Java alone? Can I skip layout in XML entirely and go straight to the source?" Yes, you can, but in practice you shouldn't. Even so, understanding how to build a layout without the XML will help you potentially modify any aspect of your layout at runtime.

VIEWS IN JAVA

Anything you can lay out or build in XML, you can lay out and build within the Java code itself; it's just more complex. It's important, however, to understand what Android is doing as it inflates and builds your layouts.

Here's what the Java code looks like to build the exact same user interface that Android generates for you in XML when you create a new project:

```
public void onCreate(Bundle savedInstanceState) {
    super.onCreate(savedInstanceState);
    setContentView(buildLayouts());
}
public View buildLayouts() {
    LinearLayout topView = new LinearLayout(this);
    LayoutParams topLayoutParams = new FrameLayout.LayoutParams(
        LayoutParams.MATCH_PARENT, LayoutParams.MATCH_PARENT);
```

```
topView.setLayoutParams(topLayoutParams);

TextView textView = new TextView(this);
LinearLayout.LayoutParams textLayoutParams = new LinearLayout.LayoutParams(
    LayoutParams.WRAP_CONTENT, LayoutParams.MATCH_PARENT);

textView.setLayoutParams(textLayoutParams);
textView.setText(R.string.hello);
topView.addView(textView);
return topView;
}
```

Let's look at what is happening in the Java code. Instead of calling setContentView on an ID from the R.java file, I'm passing it an instance that the LinearLayout object returned from the buildLayouts method. In the buildLayouts method, I'm first creating a new LinearLayout (passing in this, which is referencing the activity) and a new LayoutParams object. To match what's in the XML, the new LayoutParam is initialized with both the width and the height set to MATCH_PARENT.

Once I have the layout parameters initialized for the top LinearLayout, I can pass them to the object with a setLayoutParams call. I've now got the LinearLayout configured, so it's time to move on to building the TextView.

This is a simple text view, so its layout parameters are very similar to those of its parent's layout. The only noticeable difference is that I'm setting the height, when creating the layout parameters, to scale to fit the natural size of the TextView. (Much more on dynamic heights and widths soon.)

Once I've told the TextView how it will be positioned in its parent layout via the layout parameters, I tell it which string I'd like to display. This string is defined in /res/values/strings.xml. The name attribute in XML determines what needs to appear after R.string for the system to locate your resource. You'll learn much more about resource management in the next section.

Last, I need to add the new TextView into the LinearLayout and then return the LinearLayout so it can be set as the main content view for the activity. Once that's finished, I have a layout constructed at runtime with Java code, which identically matches the layout provided by the system in XML form.

The Java code looks fairly straightforward, but XML is a much better idea for working with the layout. Using XML, you can use Android's resource management system and give non-software engineers the ability to modify the application UI.

You are always required to give a height and width for every view in your hierarchy. You may use, for these definitions in particular, five different values. They are:

- `wrap_content` (XML) / `WRAP_CONTENT` (Java) makes the view big enough to match what it contains. This might mean different things to different views, but the concept remains the same.

- `match_parent` (XML) / `MATCH_PARENT` (Java) means that I want the dimensions of this view to match the dimensions of my parent view. (In a previous iteration of Android, this was known as `fill_parent`.)

- `dip` or `dp` stands for device-independent pixels. This is a value that will give you a consistent spacing regardless of the screen density (pixels per inch) of the device. On the Nexus 1 or Nexus S, 1 dp ~= 1.5 pixels.

- `sp` stands for scaled pixel and is used for font sizing. If the user's font settings are normal, 1sp is equivalent to 1dp. `sp` lets the system know that this value can be scaled for accessibility reasons (like changing the font size).

- `px` stands for pixels. There are times when exact pixel values are necessary. I advise against using this to declare screen locations, but it's an option.

ALTERING THE UI AT RUNTIME

It's one thing to use XML or Java to define the pile of views that compose your user interface. But particularly in the XML case, you'll want to be able to retrieve and alter views with data acquired over the network, from the user, or from any other information source. Android provides a simple method for gaining access to the views that currently compose your screens by calling `findViewById`, which is an `Activity` class method.

IDENTIFYING YOUR VIEWS

Before you can find one of your views at runtime, you'll need to give it an ID. Once you've called `setContentView` on an activity, you can call `findViewById` to retrieve your views and then alter them. This process should look at least a little bit familiar, because you saw it in the previous chapter. Here's what it looks like in XML:

```
<TextView
    android:id="@+id/text_holder"
    android:layout_width="match_parent"
    android:layout_height="wrap_content"
    android:text="@string/hello" />
```

In this case, I've added an `android:id` line to name the `TextView`. The `@+` notation tells Android that rather than referring to a view, you'd like to create an ID for the view. The first reference to any ID must start with `@+id`. Subsequent references to that ID will start simply with `@id`.

Android keeps the name-spaces of its own reserved IDs. For example, if you're creating a layout to be used by `ListActivity` (an activity specifically designed to show lists of information) or a `ListFragment` (a fragment specifically showing a list), you'll want to set the ID of the `ListView` in your layout file to `"android:id="@id/android:list"`. These well-known IDs allow Android's system code to correctly find and interact with the list view that you specify. I'll provide you with more on this subject in Chapter 5, which covers list creation and management.

If you're creating a view at runtime, simply call `setId` and pass in an integer, and you'll be able to retrieve it later.

FINDING YOUR RESOURCES WITH ANDROID

When Android compiles your project, it assigns a number value for your new static numeric ID. It places this new ID in the `R.java` file within your project. This file is your gateway to everything you've defined inside the `res` folder. For every ID, layout, drawable, string, and style (and a host of other things), Android places a subsequent statically defined `int` into the R file that identifies those things. Anytime you add a line to your layout XML defining a new ID (for example, `android:id="@+id/my_new_id"`), you'll find that the next time you compile your project, you'll have an entry in the `R.id` class. In the previous example, this entry would be `R.id.my_new_id`.

RETRIEVING A VIEW

Getting the existing instance of an Android view is as simple as calling `findViewById` and passing in the ID value found in the `R.java` file. Given the earlier XML example, here's how you would grab an instance of the text view and modify its contents.

```
public void onCreate(Bundle savedInstanceState) {
    super.onCreate(savedInstanceState);
    setContentView(R.layout.main);
    TextView tv = (TextView)findViewById(R.id.text_holder);
    tv.setText(R.string.hello);
}
```

If you have been reading this book in order, this should look eerily familiar. I'm retrieving an instance of the text view as described by the layout XML. Remember that calling `findViewById` only works after you've called `setContentView` within the `onCreate` method.

KEEPING YOUR VIEWS AROUND

Calling `findViewById` will return an object that persists for the duration of your activity. This means you can add private data members to your `Activity` class to reduce the number of times you need to reach into the view hierarchy and find them. If you modify a view only once or twice during the lifetime of your activity, this trick won't save you much time, but it can save significant time if you're making frequent updates to multiple views on a very complex screen.

It's a very bad idea, however, to make changes to your views once your activity's onDestroy method has been invoked by the system. Making changes to a view that was once part of an expired activity will have dire consequences (force close dialogs, grumpy users, bad market reviews).

XML VS. JAVA LAYOUTS

On the whole, laying out your view in Java is nearly as simple as writing it out in XML. So why would you put any layouts in XML? The short answer includes the following:

- **Resource resolution.** Android has a very powerful resource resolution system in place to choose the appropriate resource based on the hardware and settings of the user's device. Resource resolution is what allows tablet users in Germany and phone users in America to use the same application. By having separate XML layouts for tablet and phone, and separate string files for English and German, Android can deliver the appropriate XML resources, and your Java code won't know the difference.

- **Keeping view and business logic separate.** By keeping your view logic separate from your business logic, you help maintain a clear division of what should go where. Building views in code programmatically is doable, but where do you draw the line on how much work those views should be doing? XML layouts help keep those divisions clear.

- **Get those designers to work!** Ask your designer to look for a Java source file and align the title TextView in the center instead of to the left. Good luck! Ask that same designer to accomplish the same task via XML, and you'll have much greater success. With the Android UI Designer, most designers can beat the XML layouts into displayable shape. Although you might be the only one working on your current project, this will not be true for all your projects.

The longer answer to the question of XML versus Java layouts will become clear as you read the "Resource Management" section.

HANDLING A FEW COMMON TASKS

Some tasks are more common than others. Let's take a look at how you can handle some of the ones that you'll do a few dozen times before you finish your first application.

CHANGING THE VISIBILITY OF A VIEW

Most of the time, if you want to define your UI in XML you'll need to add views that will be visible only some of the time.

> **TIP:** If you find yourself doing this a lot, be sure to check out the ViewStub class.

Depending on how dynamic your application is, views come and go fairly regularly. Showing and hiding views is as simple as using the ever-trusty findViewById and then calling setVisibility on the returned object:

```
Button button = (Button)findViewById(R.id.sample_button);
//Cycle through the View Visibility settings
//Gone (no impact on layouts, essentially not there)
button.setVisibility(View.GONE);
//Invisible (holds its space in a layout but is not drawn)
button.setVisibility(View.INVISIBLE);
//Visible (duh)
button.setVisibility(View.VISIBLE);
```

This code has three visibility settings. GONE and VISIBLE are the most obvious. You'll find yourself using INVISIBLE less often, but it's great for keeping all the other views inside your layouts from moving around when you want to hide something.

SETTING AN ONCLICKLISTENER

Setting up a listener to tell you that one of your views has been clicked is one of the most common tasks you'll do when working on an Android application. Your click listener will be called if the user taps a finger down on your view and then lifts up with the finger still within the bounds of the view. This is an important distinction: Your click listener will not be invoked when a finger actually clicks down on the view but rather when the user lifts the finger up. This gives the user the chance to put a finger down in the wrong place and then correct the position before lifting it.

You can track view clicks in several ways. You can declare that your activity itself implements the view's OnClickListener interface, add a public void onClick (View v) method, and pass a reference to your activity to the view you wish to track. Here's what that looks like in code for theoretical buttons with IDs button_one and button_two declared in an imaginary main.xml layout file:

```
public class UiDemoActivity extends Activity implements OnClickListener {

    @Override
    public void onCreate(Bundle savedInstanceState) {
        super.onCreate(savedInstanceState);
        setContentView(R.layout.main);
        Button buttonOne = (Button)findViewById(R.id.button_one);
        if(buttonOne != null)
            buttonOne.setOnClickListener(this);
        Button buttonTwo = (Button)findViewById(R.id.button_two);
        if(buttonTwo!= null)
            buttonTwo.setOnClickListener(this);
    }
```

```
    @Override
    public void onClick(View selectedView) {
        if(selectedView.getId() == R.id.button_one){
            //Take Button One actions
        }
        if(selectedView.getId() == R.id.button_one){
            //Take Button Two actions
        }
    }
}
```

There are two methods at work here. In the onCreate method that is called when the activity is being initialized, you'll see me pulling button_one and button_two out of the layout with findViewById. If the system correctly returned an instance, I register my activity (passing in a reference to the activity with this) as the click listener for each view.

Registering a click listener with a view does two things. First, it tells the system to call the appropriate onClick method. Second, it tells the system that this view accepts both focus (highlightable by the navigation buttons) and touch events. You can switch these states on or off by yourself with code, but setting a click listener ensures that click events can actually be *heard* by the view.

There's a second way to set up the same dynamic. This method sets up a new OnClick Listener object for each view. This can help keep code separate if your screen has a lot of clickable items on it. Here's what this pattern looks like, and it achieves the same results as the previous code:

```
public class UiDemoActivity extends Activity{

    @Override
    public void onCreate(Bundle savedInstanceState) {
        super.onCreate(savedInstanceState);
        setContentView(R.layout.main);
        Button buttonOne = (Button)findViewById(R.id.button_one);
        if(buttonOne != null)
            buttonOne.setOnClickListener(mClickListenerOne);
        Button buttonTwo = (Button)findViewById(R.id.button_two);
        if(buttonTwo!= null)
            buttonTwo.setOnClickListener(mClickListenerTwo);
    }

    private View.OnClickListener mClickListenerOne =
        new View.OnClickListener() {
```

```
        @Override
        public void onClick(View v) {
            //Do button one stuff here
        }
    };
    private View.OnClickListener mClickListenerTwo =
        new View.OnClickListener() {
        @Override
        public void onClick(View v) {
            //Do button two stuff here
        }
    };
}
```

This time, instead of declaring my activity as an implementer of the OnClickListener, I'm creating two separate anonymous inner class objects to handle the click event from each individual button. I'll put the code required for button_one in the first object and the code for button_two in the second. I do this frequently in my own applications when I have several buttons on the screen. It keeps me from having a heaping pile of if statements (or one switch statement) that figure out which view was clicked and then take the appropriate action.

Depending on your needs, you can mix and match the two techniques. There isn't a huge advantage either way, but it's good to know each so you can keep your code in good order.

In this example, I've added a click listener to two buttons. A click listener can be attached to any view that you want users to interact with. This can be anything from entire view groups to simple text views.

It's worth mentioning again that by setting a click listener, you're telling the system that the item can be selected (touched with a finger) and potentially even clicked (highlighted with the trackpad and then clicked with the center key or trackball). As a result, whatever default selection action is configured for the view will run automatically on a select event (either from the directional keypad or the touchscreen). Buttons, for example, change colors when a user selects them. Text views, depending on the device's default UI style, may also change the active color of the text. In the end, you can (and probably should) specify custom display behavior by declaring a selector drawable. I'll show you how to do such things later in the book.

CREATING CUSTOM VIEWS

The concept of custom views can be broken out into two sections: extending an existing view and creating an entirely new one. I've rarely, in my career as an Android developer, created a completely custom view, so we'll skip over it here. The Android SDK documentation has directions for the industrious among you who want to roll your very own from scratch. However, even if you plan to extend an Android view, you must create a new class that extends the existing view. Here's how you'd go about it.

DECLARING THE NEW CLASS

The first step in declaring a custom view is to create the class. Android allows you to subclass any of its existing UI objects by simply extending an existing class. The declaration looks like this:

```
public class CustomTextView extends TextView{
    public CustomTextView(Context context) {
        super(context);
    }
}
```

That's all it takes to create a custom text view. However, since there's about as much custom in this custom text view as there is beef in fast-food tacos, I'll add something simple to set it apart.

EXTENDING A VIEW

Although Android's layouts and views are powerful and versatile, there are times when they just won't do exactly what you want. Fortunately, their functionality is easy to extend. To demonstrate, I've written a custom text view that changes the color of every letter in the text to be displayed onscreen. While this isn't the most practical use case, it will show how simple it is to implement your own behavior.

CUSTOMIZING AN EXTENDED VIEW

You'd be amazed at how much code it takes to correctly render text to the screen. Android's TextView.java class is over 9000 lines of code. But thanks to the ability to extend a class, you can use all the complex layout code and customize only the part that appeals to you. In this example, I catch the text as it changes and add a new ForegroundColorSpan for each letter in the new string. First, I declare an array of colors.

```
public class CustomTextView extends TextView{
    int colorArray[] = new int[]{Color.WHITE,
        Color.RED,
        Color.YELLOW,
        Color.GREEN,
        Color.BLUE,
        Color.MAGENTA,
        Color.CYAN,
        Color.DKGRAY};
```

Now, each time the text changes, I add a new ForegroundColorSpan for each letter.

```
protected void onTextChanged(CharSequence text,
        int start, int before, int after )
{
    //Keep the view from getting into an infinite loop
```

```
   if(selfChange){
      selfChange = false;
      return;
   }
   selfChange=true;
}
```

I make sure I don't get stuck in an infinite loop (with the change in color triggering another onTextChanged call, which changes the color again, which changes the color... you get the idea). Next comes the code that changes the colors:

```
SpannableStringBuilder builder = new SpannableStringBuilder(text);
builder.clearSpans();
ForegroundColorSpan colorSpan;
int color;
for(int i=0; i < text.length(); i++){
   //pick the next color
   color = colorArray[i%colorArray.length];
   //Create the color span
   colorSpan = new ForegroundColorSpan(color);
   //Add the color span for this one char
   builder.setSpan(colorSpan,i, i,
          Spannable.SPAN_EXCLUSIVE_EXCLUSIVE);
}
setText(builder);
```

Again, not very complex, but then neither is extending an existing view class. Also, be warned that this code will clear any formatting that may have already been set on the text. (At this point, don't stress too much about how spans and SpannableStringBuilders work. In short, they're blocks of formatting that you can drop over strings. Check the Android SDK documentation for more info.) If you're looking for a coding challenge, try creating an array with every possible RGB hex color value and cycling through that array.

USING YOUR EXTENDED VIEW

Just as with any other Android view, you can create a new instance of it at runtime in your Java code or pre-declare it in your XML layout file. Here's how you can use it in your activity:

```
public void onCreate(Bundle savedInstanceState) {
   super.onCreate(savedInstanceState);
   CustomTextView customView = new CustomTextView(this);
   customView.setText("Hello There!");
   setContentView(customView);
}
```

I'm creating a new instance of my view, setting the text for it, and then setting it as the main view for my activity. You could also put it inside a layout object with other views. It's also possible to add this custom view to an XML-described layout. But before you can start declaring your custom view in an XML file, you need to create the full suite of View constructors. Your custom view should look something like this:

```java
public class CustomTextView extends TextView{
    public CustomTextView(Context context,
            AttributeSet attributeSet,
            int defSytle) {
        super(context, attributeSet, defSytle);
    }
    public CustomTextView(Context context,
            AttributeSet attributeSet) {
        super(context, attributeSet);
    }

    public CustomTextView(Context context){
        super(context);
    }
    //Rest of the class omitted for brevity
}
```

When Android parses your XML layout and creates your view, it needs to pass an attribute set to the constructor because this contains all the layout information, text, and whatever else you've added that starts with android. If you forget to add these, everything will compile, but it will show the Unexpected Force Close window of doom when you try to draw the screen.

Now that you have the correct constructors, it's possible to create and lay out your custom view within XML. In the code that follows, I've added a single instance of the rainbow animating custom text display.

```xml
<?xml version="1.0" encoding="utf-8"?>
<LinearLayout xmlns:android="http://schemas.android.com/apk/res/
    android"
    android:orientation="vertical"
    android:layout_width="match_parent"
    android:layout_height="match_parent" >

    <com.peachpit.ui.CustomTextView
        android:layout_width="wrap_content"
        android:layout_height="wrap_content"
        android:text="See how the colors change!" />
```

As you can see, adding a custom text view to your XML layouts only requires you to use the full Java package and class name. You can also see that because `CustomTextView` extends `TextView`, I can use any attribute (like `android:text`) that I would use with one of Android's `TextViews`.

Congrats, you've created a custom Android view to do your bidding in only a few lines of code, you've displayed it to the screen, and you even have the capability to include it within a more complex layout system. Google has done a fantastic job of allowing developers to extend the functionality of the basic building blocks included in the Android SDK. If this extended custom view leaves you wanting more of a challenge, try making a simple text view that does exactly the same things as the extended view. You'll need to explore the `onMeasure` and `onDraw` methods of your own view. Go ahead, check it out; I'll be here when you get back.

RESOURCE MANAGEMENT

Android has many tools to help you manage string literals, images, layouts, and more. Moving all this constant data into external files makes life as a programmer easier in a multitude of ways. In previous code examples, I've referenced the `R.java` file when specifying strings, drawable images, and layouts and mentioned that an explanation would be forthcoming. Now is the time to explain Android resource management in detail.

RESOURCE FOLDER OVERVIEW

Every Android project, by default, contains a `res` folder with several subfolders inside it. Each subfolder is responsible for a different aspect of your application's data.

The drawable folders (`drawable-xhdpi`, `drawable-hdpi`, `drawable-mdpi`, and so on) hold images and XML files describing drawable objects. You'll learn much more about what you can do with drawable objects in later chapters.

The `values` folder holds all your textual content, from string literals to menu list value arrays to color constants.

Lastly, the layout folders contain XML files to describe how you want your screens to look.

At compile time, the Android tools take all the folders in your `res` directory and place a corresponding ID into an `R.java` file. This file is re-created and placed automatically in the project's gen (Eclipse) or `build` (Android Studio) folder. Consequently, you should never directly change this `R.java` file, because any changes are removed the next time you compile. The IDs in `R.java` can be passed to everything from XML parsers to text and image views. When you call `setText` on a `TextView` and pass in `R.string.hello`, the view then knows to look for that ID in the string file and display what it finds there. When you set the main view of an activity by calling `setContentView` and passing in `R.layout.main`, the system knows that it needs to inflate and create the views found in `res/layout/main.xml` and add them to the active views on the screen for the current activity.

Here's what the R.java file looks like for a newly created project:

```
/* AUTO-GENERATED FILE. DO NOT MODIFY.
 *
 * This class was automatically generated by the
 * aapt tool from the resource data it found. It
 * should not be modified by hand.
 */
package com.peachpit;
public final class R {
   public static final class attr {
   }
   public static final class drawable {
      public static final int icon=0x7f020000;
   }
   public static final class layout {
      public static final int main=0x7f030000;
   }
   public static final class string {
      public static final int app_name=0x7f040001;
      public static final int hello=0x7f040000;
   }
}
```

When Android compiles your XML files, it renders them to a packed binary format. The upside of this format is that it loads much faster, so your screens can snap into focus more quickly. The downside is that you cannot modify any of these files once they've been compiled. So you can't manipulate your layout and string files at runtime. You can, however, modify what is rendered to the screen by loading and changing strings in the Java representation of the views.

Additionally, if you want to reference various resources from other XML files, you'll use the @folder/object_id structure. While you may not have been aware of it, you've seen this kind of declaration in action already. Think back to the initial Hello World layout that the Android tools provide for you. In it, you saw a text view with the following line: android:text="@string/hello". This was Android's resource system at work. Instead of specifying R.string.hello, you'll use the XML's @string/hello for XML.

Each type of folder (drawable, layout, values, and several more) has special naming conventions and tricks you can use to battle the time-consuming problems of device diversity, language localization, and differing screen resolutions and densities. Let's look at what you can do with each type of file.

VALUES FOLDER

The prospect of putting all the constant values for your user interface (strings, colors, or int/string arrays) in a separate file might sound annoying at first (especially when you consider that all text manipulators will take a resource ID or a CharSequence). However, it can cut down many days of work when translating your application to different languages.

Having all your strings in an external XML file also means that your nontechnical colleagues (product managers, designers, or micromanaging bosses) can manipulate the display text in the screens, menus, and pop-up dialogs without bothering you. This assumes, of course, that you teach them how to compile and run the project; feel free to share the first chapter of this book with them.

The values folder can contain:

- **Strings.** All string literals should go into your strings.xml file.
- **Arrays.** There is a file for the XML-defined arrays, but string arrays can still go in the strings.xml file if you don't feel like using a separate file.
- **Colors.** colors.xml can contain any number of declared color constants for use in everything from text fonts to layout backgrounds. Unless you're planning on doing a lot of custom UI drawing, this file will probably not be very large.
- **Dimensions.** dimens.xml can contain any number of possible size values used elsewhere in your layouts. This file is particularly handy if you wish to make a view taller or shorter based on the display size of the device your application is being displayed on. This might seem like a simple thing to do, but it can be very powerful when combined with the layout folders.
- **Styles.** styles.xml... yeah... more about this later.

You can create new values folders for each language by using the two-letter ISO639-2 suffix for a particular language as a suffix to values. You can, for example, create a values-es folder containing a Spanish version of the strings.xml file. When a user sets his or her phone to Spanish, Android will check automatically for an R.string.hello value defined in the strings.xml file within the new values-es folder. If it finds one, it will display the values-es version rather than the default. If it doesn't find a Spanish translation, it will default to the value you defined in values/strings.xml.

In this way, Android provides you with an easy way to localize all the strings in your application. It does, however, require you to be vigilant about placing your string literals in the strings.xml file rather than just calling setText("Text like this"); or using android:text="Text like this" in your XML.

LAYOUT FOLDERS

I'm going to give you three guesses as to what exactly goes into the layout folders. Typically, it's where you place either layout XML files for use in setContentView calls, or sublayouts that can be included via ViewStubs or inherited views (two tools that allow you to reuse views in different layouts). Android builds a helpful mechanic into the layout folders.

You can have many folders, with different suffixes, that describe how you want the application to appear under various screen configurations.

The simplest example is a layout folder and a layout-land folder. If you place a firstscreen.xml file in both folders, Android will use the one that most closely resembles the current screen mode. If you keep the android:id settings consistent, you will be able to specify two completely different-looking screens within your XML markups and interact with any of them via your Java code. This technique is complicated, so let's look at an example.

Let's say you create portrait and landscape layouts for the first screen of your application. Both files are called firstscreen.xml, and the portrait version goes in the layout folder while the landscape version goes in the layout-land folder. You could also put the portrait version in a folder named layout-port. In both versions of firstscreen.xml, you provide all the appropriate IDs for the text views, buttons, and images.

If your screen had an OK button, you'd provide the portrait and landscape versions of these buttons the same ID: R.id.ok_button. Remember that you gain access to views by calling findViewById() and passing in the ID you specified on the android:id="@+id/id_goes_here" line. In this case, if you wanted to set a click listener, you'd fetch the OK button by calling findViewById(R.id.ok_button);, and Android would return the button from your portrait screen if you're in portrait mode and the landscape version of the button if you're in landscape mode. Your code knows what it must do when that button is pressed, but it doesn't know about the dimensions or location of the button. Welcome to the happy land of the Model-View-Controller (MVC).

MVC is your number one friend when handling the diversity in device screen sizes. You can lay out your views in any possible configuration, and as long as the IDs match, you'll need to write only a single Activity class to handle all possible screen permutations. You can have specific folders, each with its own set of layout files for different screen sizes (layout-small to layout-xlarge) and densities (layout-ldpi to layout-xxhdpi), and you can mix and match. For example, layout-large-land would specify layouts for large screens (VGA and WVGA) that are in landscape mode. For the exact order in which Android defaults through the folders, be sure to check the Android SDK documentation.

I'm only scratching the surface of the possibilities that these layout folders put at your disposal. You'll learn more about this topic in coming chapters on dealing with display and hardware diversity.

DRAWABLE FOLDERS

For Android, a *drawable* is simply something that can be drawn to the screen. Android abstracts away the differences between colors, shapes, and images and allows you to deal with a superclass that can represent any number of them: Drawable.

You keep the definitions for these objects in the drawable folders.

You should consider using a drawable for two main types of objects:

- Image resources (mostly PNG files)
- XML files describing things you want drawn: shapes, gradients, or colors

The drawable set of folders works similarly to the layout folders. You can specify any mix of screen densities, layouts, or resolutions, provided you specify them in the right order.

TIP: Be sure to check the Android SDK documentation for more information on ordering your suffixes correctly.

Referencing a drawable is accomplished in the same way that you reference values and layouts. For XML files, use @drawable/resource_name. For example, in an ImageView (android:src="@drawable/bridge"), omit the suffix if you're referring to XML files or images. Also, keep in mind that Android will always try to use the drawable folder that is closest to your current configuration. If it can't find a good match, it'll cascade back to what it can find in the default drawable folder.

LAYOUT MANAGEMENT

Layouts, from the simple to the complex, describe how to arrange a complex series of views. This section covers the basics of Android's arsenal of layout classes starting with the ViewGroup, moving through LinearLayouts, and ending with the king of the Android screen arrangers, the RelativeLayout.

THE VIEWGROUP

Each layout in Android extends what's known as the ViewGroup. This is the class of views that by definition can contain other views as children.

To demonstrate how each of the major layouts function, I'll be laying out an example picture-viewer screen. While this probably won't be the most beautiful photo viewer, it will be simple and an excellent vehicle for showing you how the various layouts work.

Figure 3.1 shows the screen that we'll be rendering using the AbsoluteLayout, the LinearLayout, and the RelativeLayout.

FIGURE 3.1 A taste of what's to come.

The example picture viewer has two sections: the button bar with title, and the image itself. The button bar contains Next and Prev buttons and a text view displaying the name of the image.

Before getting too deep into the layout, there are a few terms to watch for in the XML:

- **dip** or **dp.** This is how Android helps you scale your screen layout to devices with different pixel densities. For example, on a high density pixel screen (HDPI), 1dp = 1.5 pixels; on an extra high density screen (XHDPI) screen, 1dp = 2 pixels; and so on. It can be annoying to constantly convert the locations onscreen to dips, but this small investment in time will pay huge dividends when you're running on a multitude of Android screens. Example: `android:padding="20dp"`.

- **px.** Use this suffix to define an absolute pixel value for the specified dimension. In most cases, you should avoid declaring the absolute pixel value and use dp. Example: `android:paddingLeft="15px"`.

- `match_parent` and `wrap_content`. Before you can draw an Android view to the screen, it must have a defined `width` and `height`. You can define either of these two values as a constant value (20dp), or you can use one of the two special height and width values, `match_parent` or `wrap_content`. Each value does exactly what you'd expect. The `match_parent` value will make the view attempt to match the dimension of its parent. The `wrap_content` value will first request the measured size of the view and then attempt to set that dimension as the layout width for the view itself.

With a few simple definitions out of the way, I can start in on the various layout classes. I'll start with one that you'll find appealing but that you should never use in practice.

THE ABSOLUTELAYOUT

The most important thing you should know about AbsoluteLayouts is that you should never use them. They are the quintessential beginner's trap. They appear to be a good idea at first (as they quickly give you exact pixel design), but they can be frustrating, require excess time laying out new screens, and cause frequent face-desk interaction. Consult your local Android expert if you experience any of these side effects while trying to use an AbsoluteLayout. They'll likely try to talk you out of this lunacy.

The AbsoluteLayout, as you might have guessed, allows you to specify exactly where on the screen you want a particular view to go. Each child of an AbsoluteLayout should have android:layout_x and android:layout_y values along with the required width and height settings.

You are probably thinking, "That sounds like a great way to make layouts look exactly the way I want them to. Why bother learning anything else when I can take my screen designs and convert them directly into pixel x/y locations?"

I thought the same thing... at first.

Here's what the AbsoluteLayout layout XML looks like:

```xml
<?xml version="1.0" encoding="utf-8"?>
<AbsoluteLayout
    xmlns:android="http://schemas.android.com/apk/res/android"
    android:layout_width="match_parent"
    android:layout_height="match_parent">
    <View
        android:background="#333333"
        android:layout_height="52dp"
        android:layout_width="match_parent"/>
    <Button
        android:id="@+id/prev"
        android:layout_width="wrap_content"
        android:layout_height="wrap_content"
        android:layout_x="5dp"
        android:layout_y="3dp"
        android:text="@string/prev_string"
android:textColor="@android:color/white" />
    <TextView
        android:id="@+id/text_view"
        android:layout_width="wrap_content"
        android:layout_height="wrap_content"
        android:layout_x="125dp"
        android:layout_y="20dp"
        android:text="Empire State Building"
```

FIGURE 3.2
AbsoluteLayout seems like a good idea at first—until you do anything else, like rotate.

```
android:textColor="@android:color/white" />
    <Button
        android:id="@+id/next"
        android:layout_width="wrap_content"
        android:layout_height="wrap_content"
        android:layout_x="293dp"
        android:layout_y="3dp"
        android:text="@string/next_string"
android:textColor="@android:color/white"/>
    <ImageView
        android:layout_width="match_parent"
        android:layout_height="468dp"
        android:layout_x="0dp"
        android:layout_y="52dp"
        android:scaleType="centerCrop"
        android:src="@drawable/empire_state_snapshot" />
</AbsoluteLayout>
```

Nothing in this layout code should look shocking. Each button, text view, and image view has x and y coordinates. This simple code arranges the views to look very similar to the original original (Figure 3.1).

But hang on, this is only one of the 20-something ways that you can consume a single layout. Let's look at what happens to this layout when switching to landscape (**Figure 3.2**).

Yikes, that looks... bad! This is no way for a screen to look on any layout. Sure, you could do an alternative layout for every portrait and landscape screen out there, but that could add weeks to your schedule, and, worse, every time you need a new screen aspect you'll have to start from scratch.

While the AbsoluteLayout can give you a pixel-perfect design, it can achieve that look only for a single screen configuration. Given that Android has many dozens of screen sizes and types spread across a huge number of physical devices, layouts like these will make your life miserable once you move beyond your initial test device.

The only way to make life harder for yourself is to use an AbsoluteLayout with its children views defined in exact pixels (px) x and y values. Not only will a screen laid out in this way break when you switch to landscape, but it'll break when you switch from, say, the Moto X to the Galaxy S4, because they each have different screen densities (XHDPI and XXHDPI, respectively).

I've included the AbsoluteLayout in this chapter because if I didn't, you might find it on your own and wonder at what a gem you'd found. This is a cautionary tale. The other layouts can be frustrating and time consuming up front, but trust me, they'll pay off in the end.

Bottom line: Don't use AbsoluteLayouts except for extremely simple cases. I could see it being used to lay out a small, sophisticated button that could then be dropped into one of the more dynamic layout classes—but please, for your own sanity, don't use this layout object unless you absolutely cannot avoid it.

THE LINEARLAYOUT

A LinearLayout is the exact opposite of the AbsoluteLayout. Within it, you'll define a series of views, and the system will size and place them dynamically on the screen in the order you've specified. This layout is, and I cannot emphasize this enough, not very good for putting views exactly where you want them. I'm saving the layout class that is best at this for last.

Here's how the original picture viewer looks when designed to work with a LinearLayout:

```
<LinearLayout
    xmlns:android="http://schemas.android.com/apk/res/android"
    android:layout_width="match_parent"
    android:layout_height="match_parent"
    android:orientation="vertical">

    <LinearLayout
        android:layout_width="match_parent"
        android:layout_height="wrap_content"
        android:background="#333333">
```

```
    android:orientation="horizontal">
    <Button
        android:id="@+id/prev"
        android:layout_width="wrap_content"
        android:layout_height="wrap_content"
        android:layout_weight="1"
        android:text="@string/prev_string"
        android:textColor="@android:color/white" />
    <TextView
        android:id="@+id/url_view"
        android:layout_width="wrap_content"
        android:layout_height="wrap_content"
        android:layout_weight="1"
        android:gravity="center_horizontal"
        android:text="Empire State Building"
        android:textColor="@android:color/white" />
    <Button
        android:id="@+id/next"
        android:layout_width="wrap_content"
        android:layout_height="wrap_content"
        android:layout_weight="1"
        android:text="@string/next_string"
        android:textColor="@android:color/white" />
</LinearLayout>
<ImageView
    android:layout_width="match_parent"
    android:layout_height="wrap_content"
    android:scaleType="centerCrop"
    android:src="@drawable/empire_state_snapshot" />
</LinearLayout>
```

Notice that there are two LinearLayouts at work in this example. The top-level layout contains the second LinearLayout object and the image to be displayed. The second LinearLayout contains the two buttons and the text of the title. Two layouts are required, in this case, because any one LinearLayout may have only one orientation.

FIGURE 3.3 The LinearLayout-based screen

FIGURE 3.4 The same layout but in landscape

Figure 3.3 shows what this example XML produces in portrait mode.

This is where Android's dynamic layouts really start to shine; take a look at what the exact same layout code looks like when the user shifts into landscape mode (**Figure 3.4**).

Not perfect, but a vast improvement over the AbsoluteLayout's version of the landscape screen.

ONE VIEW MUST BE IN CHARGE OF SIZE

One view, or layout, must define a height and width value. You cannot tell Android that you'd like a layout to wrap its content while, at the same time, telling a view that it should match its parent. This will cause a compile error because Android has no idea how big to make either the parent view or the child layout. Something must define an actual height, even if it's an image or a line of text.

USING LINEARLAYOUTS

When using the LinearLayout, the order in which you define your views is the order in which they're placed on the screen. First, take a look at that second LinearLayout:

```
<LinearLayout
    android:id="@+id/button_bar"
    android:layout_width="match_parent"
    android:layout_height="wrap_content"
    android:background="#333333"
    android:orientation="horizontal">
```

By setting the orientation to horizontal, Android knows to place the children in order from left to right across the top of the screen. The outer layout is a vertical one, allowing placement of the button bar above the image.

By setting the width to match_parent, I'm making sure the layout itself stretches all the way across the parent layout (in this case the entire screen). The height is set to wrap_content, so it will be exactly as tall as the final measured height of its children.

The LinearLayout distributes its children in the order they're defined. It then measures all the child views to see how much space they'd like to take up. It will then divvy up the available space in proportion to the ideal size of its children. If there is too little space to accommodate all the child views, it'll give each child a part of their required space in proportion to their measured size. If there's more than enough space for all the child views, it'll pass out the extra space based on how large the child's onMeasure call tells the layout it wants to be. You can modify this proportional distribution through the layout_weight attribute in each child.

Layout really happens more in the definition of the children than in the declaration of the layout itself. So, for a bit of context, let's take a look at the individual members of the button bar layout.

FIGURE 3.5 Overly large buttons thanks to the LinearLayout

Here is the first of the child views in the definition for the Prev button:

```
<Button
    android:id="@+id/prev"
    android:layout_width="wrap_content"
    android:layout_height="wrap_content"
    android:layout_weight="1"
    android:text="@string/prev_string"
    android:textColor="@android:color/white" />
```

The layout_weight value, which can be any number, decimal, or integer, tells the system how much space to give to the child view when the layout has either too much or too little space. The total weight distributed is the ratio of all the weights added together.

Take a look at the landscape version of the button bar again (**Figure 3.5**).

This may be very close to the way the screen looks in portrait mode, but not close enough. As the top bar grows, the LinearLayout hands out extra pixel space in proportion to the measured size of the child view. In this case, because all three elements (two buttons and the text title) are weighted the same (1), the layout divides the extra space evenly among them. You can re-weight the buttons such that they grow in different ratios to the text title. Since you want the buttons to grow at a slower rate than the text, you could try setting their weights to 0. Here is what the new values look like (with everything else omitted):

```
<LinearLayout>
    <Button
        android:layout_weight="0" />
    <TextView
        android:layout_weight="1" />
    <Button
```

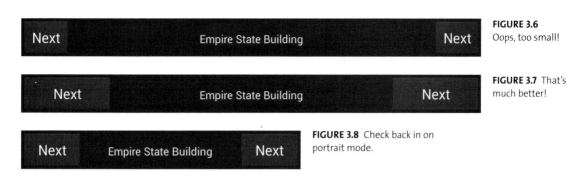

FIGURE 3.6
Oops, too small!

FIGURE 3.7 That's
much better!

FIGURE 3.8 Check back in on
portrait mode.

```
        android:layout_weight="0" />
</LinearLayout>
```

Figure 3.6 shows what this change does to the button bar.

Well, technically that's correct, but it looks awful. You have two options. You can declare exactly how much extra space you'd like each of the two buttons to have through the `android:padding` declaration, or you can give them a little bit more weight. You can fiddle with the first option on your own, but let's take a look at the padding option together.

Although you don't want the buttons to get too large, you still need to give them a bit more space than exactly what fits around the text. Let's try .25 for a `weight`. I've pulled out all non-`layout_weight` lines for brevity:

```
<LinearLayout>
    <Button
        android:layout_weight=".25" />
    <TextView
        android:layout_weight="1" />
    <Button
        android:layout_weight=".25" />
</LinearLayout>
```

Figure 3.7 shows how that looks in landscape mode.

The result is much more reasonable. But to be sure, check what the bar looks like in portrait mode. **Figure 3.8** shows the result.

Perhaps the Next and Prev buttons could be a little bit larger in portrait mode, but this result is more than acceptable. They're not huge, they don't look crowded, and they should be big enough for even large fingers to hit.

In the end, nothing beats the `LinearLayouts` for easily handling different dynamic screen sizes. Throw as much into one as you please, and it'll try to accommodate everything. There are, however, two major issues to watch out for. First, because they can orient themselves in only one direction, you may end up needing a lot of them to handle a complex layout, which can slow drawing performance significantly. Second, getting a complex screen to render exactly as your designer wants it to can be an intensive process. For more complex or busy screens and objects, you're much better off using a `RelativeLayout`.

FIGURE 3.9
Designing the same
screen, but with the
RelativeLayout.

THE RELATIVELAYOUT

The RelativeLayout is the king of the Android screen layout system. It allows you to position all your child views in relation to either the parent (the layout itself) or any other child view within the layout. Let's take a look at one in action. Here's the now familiar image and button arrangement in the photo viewer, but with a RelativeLayout (**Figure 3.9**).

There are a few slight measurement differences between this image and the one produced with the LinearLayout. This one is also missing the gray background behind the buttons, which I'll show you how to add shortly.

Take a look at the XML layout that produced the image in Figure 3.9.

```
<?xml version="1.0" encoding="utf-8"?>
<RelativeLayout
    xmlns:android="http://schemas.android.com/apk/res/android"
    android:layout_width="match_parent"
    android:layout_height="match_parent">
    <View
        android:layout_width="match_parent"
        android:layout_height="wrap_content"
        android:background="#333333"
```

```
        android:layout_alignBottom="@+id/next"
        android:layout_alignParentTop="true" />
    <Button
        android:id="@+id/prev"
        android:layout_width="wrap_content"
        android:layout_height="wrap_content"
        android:layout_alignParentLeft="true"
        android:layout_alignParentTop="true"
        android:text="@string/prev_string"
        android:textColor="@android:color/white" />
    <Button
        android:id="@+id/next"
        android:layout_width="wrap_content"
        android:layout_height="wrap_content"
        android:layout_alignParentRight="true"
        android:layout_alignParentTop="true"
        android:text="@string/next_string"
        android:textColor="@android:color/white" />
    <TextView
        android:id="@+id/text_view"
        android:layout_width="wrap_content"
        android:layout_height="wrap_content"
        android:gravity="center"
        android:layout_toLeftOf="@id/next"
        android:layout_toRightOf="@id/prev"
        android:layout_alignBottom="@id/prev"
        android:layout_alignTop="@id/prev"
        android:text="Empire State Building"
        android:textColor="@android:color/white" />
    <ImageView
        android:layout_width="match_parent"
        android:layout_height="wrap_content"
        android:layout_below="@id/prev"
    android:scaleType="centerCrop"
        android:src="@drawable/empire_state_snapshot" />
</RelativeLayout>
```

NOTE: If you reference an "@id/..." for layout purposes, before the view is declared in XML you need to declare it with an "@+id/...". Otherwise, your compiler will complain that it doesn't see the ID you're referencing.

In this layout code, you see the same view components that made up the LinearLayout, but with the relative version, there's no need for a second, nested layout. The mechanics to each member of a RelativeLayout can be more complex than its linear cousin, so I'll break down all four pieces of this screen one at a time.

The <RelativeLayout> declaration contains only enough information to tell the layout to fill the entire screen. All information on how to lay out the screen is found in the child elements. Here's the first one:

```
<Button
    android:id="@+id/prev"
    android:layout_width="wrap_content"
    android:layout_height="wrap_content"
    android:layout_alignParentLeft="true"
    android:layout_alignParentTop="true"
    android:text="@string/prev_string"
    android:textColor="@android:color/white" />
```

The first view, which declares the Prev button, initially declares its ID in the android:id line. The Prev button needs an ID so you can assign a click listener to it in the activity code. The layout height and width declarations simply tell the view to make it large enough to accommodate all the content (in this case, the "prev" text and a little padding).

The padding declaration tells the system to push the boundaries for the button out from the smallest required space for the text. In this case, android:padding="15dp" tells the system to measure the required space for the "prev" text and then 15 more device-independent pixels to the outer boundary of the view. As a general rule, it's always good to pad your buttons between 10 and 20 dp (depending on screen and text size). This gives them a little more space to be recognized as buttons, and it also gives people with large fingers a chance of actually hitting the view.

Now come the parts that tell the system where inside the layout object to place the button. The attribute android:layout_alignParentLeft="true" tells Android to align the left edge of the view with the left edge of the parent's bounding rectangle. In this case, it's the left edge of the screen. The android:layout_alignParentTop="true" attribute does the same thing except with respect to the top of the layout object (in this case, the top of the application's available space).

If you don't specify any layout parameters, views will default to the upper-left corner of the layout object. This code example declares these views for explanation purposes.

Now that the Prev button is in place, you're ready to move on. Here's the relevant XML for the Next button:

```
<Button
    android:id="@+id/next"
    android:layout_width="wrap_content"
    android:layout_height="wrap_content"
```

```
android:layout_alignParentRight="true"
android:layout_alignParentTop="true"
android:text="@string/next_string"
android:textColor="@android:color/white" />
```

The Next button is nearly identical to the Prev button except for the ID (required to set up a click listener in the activity), the text displaying on the button ("next"), and the `android:layout_alignParentRight="true"` attribute (to lock it to the right side of the layout object—and thus the right side of the screen—instead of the left). Here's the code for the title:

```
<TextView
    android:id="@+id/text_view"
    android:layout_width="wrap_content"
    android:layout_height="wrap_content"
    android:gravity="center"
    android:layout_toLeftOf="@id/next"
    android:layout_toRightOf="@id/prev"
    android:layout_alignBottom="@id/prev"
    android:layout_alignTop="@id/prev"
    android:text="Empire State Building"
    android:textColor="@android:color/white" />
```

In this text view, things start to get a little more interesting. Again, the ID, height, and width are things you've seen before, but you need to change the title text as the images change. As the image changes, you'll need an ID so the activity can change the name of the picture displayed above it.

`android:layout_toRightOf="@id/prev"` tells the layout to align the left edge of the text view with the right edge of the Prev button. `android:layout_toLeftOf= "@id/next"` tells the right edge of the text view to align with the left-most edge of the Next button. The `android:gravity="center"` attribute tells the text to center itself within any extra available space. This will center it vertically (so it doesn't stick to the top of the screen) and horizontally (so it doesn't stick against the left-most button).

This technique of centering a view in the space between two objects is one I use frequently in my Android work, and it's a good way to eat up extra space caused by small and large fluctuations in screen size. That is, the text in the center of the buttons will float, centered, within any available screen space you might get when using a larger screen than the one you're designing.

ADDING THAT GRAY BACKGROUND

So, you might be asking, if the LinearLayout example has such an easy way to add the gray background, why does the RelativeLayout need an extra view? First, stop asking your book questions; you'll look a little odd in public. Second, I've put it in this way so you can see that sometimes, even though you can do it all in one way, the best solutions are a mix of both:

```
<!-- This is the top level layout -->
<RelativeLayout
    xmlns:android="http://schemas.android.com/apk/res/android"
    android:layout_width="match_parent"
    android:layout_height="match_parent">
    <View
        android:layout_width="match_parent"
        android:layout_height="wrap_content"
        android:background="#333333"
        android:layout_alignBottom="@+id/next"
        android:layout_alignParentTop="true" />

    <!--Rest of the screen goes here -->
</RelativeLayout>
```

I want the gray box to be drawn behind the button bar, so I placed it as the first view in the layout. Android draws the view stack in the order they're declared. So, were I to incorrectly place the listed XML below the button and text declarations, you'd see only the gray bar covering over both the text and the buttons.

The key attribute here is `layout_alignBottom`, which will align the bottom of the view with the bottom of the view that has the ID you give it. This same property works with `layout_alignTop`, `layout_alignLeft`, and `layout_alignRight`.

With that, you've successfully added a gray background and brought the `RelativeLayout` version of this view into parity with the earlier `LinearLayout` demonstration. The `Relative Layout` can handle more complex displays without requiring other nested layouts. It also can, if you're smart about it, handle changes in screen size, as shown by having the image's name float between the buttons no matter how far apart they get.

WITH GREAT POWER COMES GREAT RESPONSIBILITY

The `RelativeLayout` is a great tool for getting things where you want them in a variety of complicated situations, but this flexibility comes at a price. As indicated before with `Linear Layout`, nesting too deeply in `RelativeLayout` can quickly turn into a performance disaster. By nature of having pieces laid out relative to each other, the system must perform multiple layout passes to determine how much space each view can take up.

It's easy to see how—if one view's left bound depends on another view's right bound, which depends on the size of the parent view, which even further depends on the gravity of its parent view—measuring these sizes can get out of hand. While I'm confident that you will always get the result you're imagining, you may also run into system failures if things get too complex.

WRAPPING UP

Throughout this chapter, you've come to understand the fundamental building blocks that make up Android's UI. While I haven't yet had time to show you any of these particular classes in much depth, together we've laid the groundwork for more serious chapters to come. In this way, I can dive deep into TextViews (yes, we will) without worrying that you won't know how to arrange them next to an image or make them respond to click events.

This concludes the overview of displaying information to users. You should be comfortable building and changing basic user interfaces through Java and Android's XML layout system. If you didn't skip any sections, you'll also be able to extend existing built-in views to make Android do exactly your bidding. Next you'll take a break from drawing things on screens and look at how to acquire data for your pretty user interfaces.

CHAPTER 4

Acquiring Data

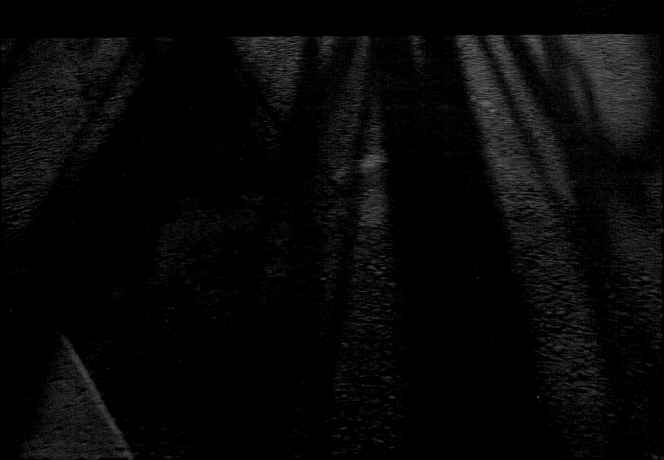

Although the prime directive of this chapter is to teach you how to acquire data from a remote source, this is really just a sneaky way for me to teach you about Android and the main thread. For the sake of simplicity, all the examples in this chapter will deal with downloading and rendering image data. In the next chapter, on adapters and lists, I'll introduce you to parsing complex data and displaying it to users. Image data, as a general rule, is larger and more cumbersome, so you'll run into more interesting and demonstrative timing issues in dealing with it.

THE MAIN THREAD

The Android operation system has exactly one blessed thread authorized to change anything that will be seen by the user. This alleviates what could be a concurrency nightmare, such as view locations and data changing in one thread while a different one is trying to lay them out onscreen. If only one thread is allowed to touch the user interface, Android can guarantee that nothing vital is changed while it's measuring views and rendering them to the screen. This has, unfortunately, serious repercussions for how you'll need to acquire and process data. Let me start with a simple example.

YOU THERE, FETCH ME THAT DATA!

Were I to ask you, right now, to download an image and display it to the screen, you'd probably write code that looks a lot like this:

```
public void onCreate(Bundle extra){
   try{
      URL url = new URL("http://wanderingoak.net/bridge.png");
      HttpURLConnection httpCon =
         (HttpURLConnection)url.openConnection();

      if(httpCon.getResponseCode() != 200) {
         throw new Exception("Failed to connect");
      }

      InputStream is = httpCon.getInputStream();
      Bitmap bitmap = BitmapFactory.decodeStream(is);
      ImageView iv = (ImageView)findViewById(R.id.main_image);
      iv.setImageBitmap(bitmap);

   }catch(Exception e){
      Log.e("ImageFetching","Didn't work!",e);
   }
}
```

This is exactly what I did when initially faced with the same problem. While this code will fetch and display the required bitmap, there is a very sinister issue lurking in the code—namely, the code itself is running on the main thread. Why is this a problem? Consider that there can be only one main thread and that the main thread is the only one that can interact with the screen in any capacity. This means that while the example code is waiting for the network to come back with image data, nothing whatsoever can be rendered to the screen.

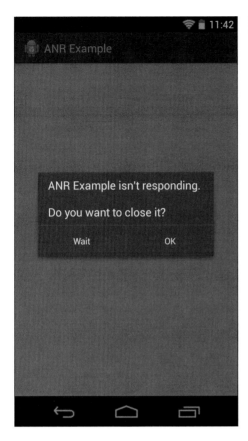

FIGURE 4.1 What the user sees when you hold the main thread hostage.

This image-fetching code will block any action from taking place anywhere on the device. If you hold the main thread hostage, buttons will not be processed, phone calls cannot be answered, and nothing can be drawn to the screen until you release it.

WATCHDOGS

Given that a simple programmer error (like the one in the example code) could effectively cripple any Android device, Google has gone to great lengths to make sure no single application can control the main thread for any length of time. Starting in Android Honeycomb (3.0), if you open any network connections on the main thread, your application will crash. If you're hogging too much of the main thread's time with long-running operations, such as calculating pi or finding the next prime number, your application will produce this disastrous dialog box (**Figure 4.1**) on top of your application.

This dialog box is unaffectionately referred to by developers as an ANR (App Not Responding) crash. Although operations will continue in the background, and the user can press the Wait button to return to whatever's going on within your application, this is catastrophic for most users, and you should avoid it at all costs.

WHAT NOT TO DO

What kind of things should you avoid on the main thread?

- Anything involving the network
- Any task requiring a read from or write to the file system
- Heavy processing of any kind (such as image or movie modification)
- Any task that blocks a thread while you wait for something to complete

Excluding this list, there isn't much left, so as a general rule, if it doesn't involve setup or modification of the user interface, *don't* do it on the main thread.

WHEN AM I ON THE MAIN THREAD?

Anytime a method is called from the system (unless explicitly otherwise stated), you can be sure you're on the main thread. Again, as a general rule, if you're not in a thread created by you, it's safe to assume you're probably on the main one, so be careful.

GETTING OFF THE MAIN THREAD

You can see why holding the main thread hostage while grabbing a silly picture of the Golden Gate Bridge is a bad idea. But how, you might be wondering, do I get off the main thread? An inventive hacker might simply move all the offending code into a separate thread. This imaginary hacker might produce code looking something like this:

```
public void onCreate(Bundle extra){
    new Thread(){
        public void run(){
            try{
                URL url = new URL("http://wanderingoak.net/bridge.png");
                HttpURLConnection httpCon =
                    (HttpURLConnection) url.openConnection();

                if(httpCon.getResponseCode() != 200){
                throw new Exception("Failed to connect");
                }

                InputStream is = httpCon.getInputStream();
                Bitmap bitmap = BitmapFactory.decodeStream(is);
                ImageView iv = (ImageView)findViewById(R.id.remote_image);
                iv.setImageBitmap(bt);
            }catch(Exception e){
                //handle failure here
            }
        }
    }.start();
}
```

"There," your enterprising hacker friend might say, "I've fixed your problem. The main thread can continue to run unimpeded by the silly PNG downloading code." There is, however, another problem with this new code. If you run the method on your own emulator, you'll see that it throws an exception and cannot display the image onscreen.

Why, you might now ask, is this new failure happening? Well, remember that the main thread is the only one allowed to make changes to the user interface. Calling setImage Bitmap is very much in the realm of one of those changes and, thus, can be done only while on the main thread.

GETTING BACK TO MAIN LAND

Android provides, through the Activity class, a way to get back on the main thread as long as you have access to an activity. Let me fix the hacker's code to do this correctly. I don't want to indent the code into the following page, so I'll show the code beginning from the line on which the bitmap is created (remember, we're still inside the Activity class, within the onCreate method, inside an inline thread declaration) (why do I hear the music from *Inception* playing in my head?).

If you're confused, check the sample code for this chapter.

```
final Bitmap bt = BitmapFactory.decodeStream(is);
ImageActivity.this.runOnUiThread(new Runnable() {
public void run() {
    ImageView iv = (ImageView)findViewById(R.id.remote_image);
      iv.setImageBitmap(bt);
      }
  });
//All the close brackets omitted to save space
```

Remember, we're already running in a thread, so accessing just this will refer to the thread itself. I, on the other hand, need to invoke a method on the activity. Calling Image Activity.this provides a reference to the outer Activity class in which we've spun up this hacky code and will thus allow us to call runOnUiThread. Further, because I want to access the recently created bitmap in a different thread, I'll need to make the bitmap declaration final or the compiler will get cranky with us.

When you call runOnUiThread, Android will schedule this work to be done as soon as the main thread is free from other tasks. Once back on the main thread, all the same "don't be a hog" rules again apply.

THERE MUST BE A BETTER WAY!

If you're looking at this jumbled, confusing, un-cancelable code and thinking to yourself, "Self. There must be a cleaner way to do this," you'd be right. There are many ways to handle long-running tasks; I'll show you what I think are the two most useful. One is the AsyncTask, a simple way to do an easy action within an activity. The other, IntentService, is more complicated but much better at handling repetitive work that can span multiple activities.

THE ASYNCTASK

At its core, the AsyncTask is an abstract class that you extend and that provides the basic framework for a time-consuming asynchronous task.

The best way to describe the AsyncTask is to call it a working thread sandwich. That is to say, it has three major methods for which you can provide implementation.

- onPreExecute takes place on the main thread and is the first slice of bread. It sets up the task, prepares a loading dialog, and warns the user that something is about to happen.
- doInBackground is the meat of this little task sandwich (and is also required). This method is guaranteed by Android to run on a separate background thread. This is where the majority of your work takes place.
- onPostExecute will be called once your work is finished (again, on the main thread), and the results produced by the background method will be passed to it. This is the other slice of bread.

That's the gist of the asynchronous task. There are more-complicated factors that I'll touch on in just a minute, but this is one of the fundamental building blocks of the Android platform (given that all hard work must be taken off the main thread).

Take a look at one in action, and then we'll go over the specifics of it:

```
private class ImageDownloader extends AsyncTask<String, Integer, Bitmap>{

    Override
    protected void onPreExecute(){
        //Setup is done here
    }

    @Override
    protected Bitmap doInBackground(String... params) {
        try{
            URL url = new URL(params[0]);
            HttpURLConnection httpCon =
        (HttpURLConnection) url.openConnection();

            if(httpCon.getResponseCode() != 200)
                throw new Exception("Failed to connect");
        }

            InputStream is = httpCon.getInputStream();
            return BitmapFactory.decodeStream(is);
```

```
    }catch(Exception e){
        Log.e("Image","Failed to load image",e);
    }
    return null;
}
@Override
protected void onProgressUpdate(Integer... params){
    //Update a progress bar here, or ignore it, it's up to you
}
@Override
protected void onPostExecute(Bitmap img){
    ImageView iv = (ImageView) findViewById(R.id.remote_image);
    if(iv!=null && img!=null){
        iv.setImageBitmap(img);
    }
}


@Override
protected void onCancelled(){
    // Handle what you want to do if you cancel this task
}
}
```

That, dear readers, is an asynchronous task that will download an image at the end of any URL and display it for your pleasure (provided you have an image view onscreen with the ID remote_image). Here is how you'd kick off such a task from the onCreate method of your activity.

```
public void onCreate(Bundle extras){
    super.onCreate(extras);
    setContentView(R.layout.image_layout);

    ImageDownloader imageDownloader = new ImageDownloader();
    imageDownloader.execute("http://wanderingoak.net/bridge.png");
}
```

Once you call execute on the ImageDownloader, it will download the image, process it into a bitmap, and display it to the screen. That is, assuming your image_layout.xml file contains an ImageView with the ID remote_image.

HOW TO MAKE IT WORK FOR YOU

The AsyncTask requires that you specify three generic type arguments (if you're unsure about Java and generics, do a little Googling before you press on) as you declare your extension of the task.

- The type of parameter that will be passed into the class. In this example AsyncTask code, I'm passing one string that will be the URL, but I could pass several of them. The parameters will always be referenced as an array no matter how many of them you pass in. Notice that I reference the single URL string as params[0].

- The object passed between the doInBackground method (*off* the main thread) and the onProgressUpdate method (which will be called *on* the main thread). It doesn't matter in the example, because I'm not doing any progress updates in this demo, but it'd probably be an integer, which would be either the percentage of completion of the transaction or the number of bytes transferred.

- The object that will be returned by the doInBackground method to be handled by the onPostExecute call. In this little example, it's the bitmap we set out to download.

Here's the line in which all three objects are declared:

```
private class ImageDownloader extends
    AsyncTask<String, Integer, Bitmap>{
```

In this example, these are the classes that will be passed to your three major methods.

ONPREEXECUTE

```
protected void onPreExecute(){
}
```

onPreExecute is usually when you'll want to set up a loading dialog or a loading spinner in the corner of the screen (I'll discuss dialogs in depth later). Remember, onPreExecute is called on the main thread, so don't touch the file system or network at all in this method.

DOINBACKGROUND

```
protected Bitmap doInBackground(String... params) {
}
```

This is your chance to make as many network connections, file system accesses, or other lengthy operations as you like without holding up the phone. The class of object passed to this method will be determined by the first generic object in your AsyncTask's class declaration. Although I'm using only one parameter in the code sample, you can actually pass any number of parameters (as long as they derive from the saved class), and you'll have them at your fingertips when doInBackground is called. Once your long-running task has been completed, you'll need to return the result at the end of your function. This final value will be passed into another method called back on the main UI thread.

SHOWING YOUR PROGRESS

There's another aspect of the AsyncTask that you should be aware of even though I haven't demonstrated it. From within doInBackground, you can send progress updates to the user interface. doInBackground isn't on the main thread, so if you'd like to update a progress bar or change the state of something on the screen, you'll have to get back on the main thread to make the change.

Within the AsyncTask, you can do this during the doInBackground method by calling publishProgress and passing in any number of objects deriving from the second class in the AsyncTask declaration (in the case of this example, an integer). Android will then, on the main thread, call your declared onProgressUpdate method and hand over any classes you passed to publishProgress. Here's what the method looks like in the AsyncTask example:

```
protected void onProgressUpdate(Integer... params){
    //Update a progress bar here, or ignore it, it's up to you
}
```

As always, be careful when doing UI updates, because if the activity isn't currently onscreen or has been destroyed, you could run into some trouble. The section "A Few Important Caveats" discusses the "bad things" that can happen.

ONPOSTEXECUTE

The work has been finished, or, as in the example, the image has been downloaded. It's time to update the screen with what I've acquired. At the end of doInBackground, if successful, I return a loaded bitmap to the AsyncTask. Now Android will switch to the main thread and call onPostExecute, passing the class I returned at the end of doInBackground. Here's what the code for that method looks like:

```
protected void onPostExecute(Bitmap img){
    ImageView iv = (ImageView)findViewById(R.id.remote_image);
    if(iv!=null && img!=null){
        iv.setImageBitmap(img);
    }
}
```

I take the bitmap downloaded from the website, retrieve the image view into which it's going to be loaded, and set it as that view's bitmap to be rendered. There's an error case I haven't correctly handled here. Take a second to look back at the original code and see if you can spot it.

A FEW IMPORTANT CAVEATS

Typically, an AsyncTask is started from within an activity. However, you must remember that activities can have short life spans. Recall that, by default, Android destroys and re-creates any activity each time you rotate the screen. Android will also destroy your activity when the user backs out of it. You might reasonably ask, "If I start an AsyncTask from within an activity and then that activity is destroyed, what happens?" You guessed it: very bad things. Trying to draw to an activity that's already been removed from the screen can cause all manner of havoc (usually in the form of unhandled exceptions).

It's a good idea to keep track of any AsyncTasks you've started, and when the activity's onDestroy method is called, make sure to call cancel on any lingering AsyncTask.

There are two cases in which the AsyncTask is perfect for the job:

- Downloading small amounts of data specific to one particular activity
- Loading files from an external storage drive (usually an SD card)

Make sure that the data you're moving with the AsyncTask pertains to only one activity, because your task generally shouldn't span more than one. You can pass it between activities if the screen has been rotated, but this can be tricky.

There are a few cases when it's not a good idea to use an AsyncTask:

- Any acquired data that may pertain to more than one activity shouldn't be acquired through an AsyncTask. Both an image that might be shown on more than one screen and a list of messages in a Twitter application, for example, would have relevance outside a single activity.

- Data to be posted to a web service is also a bad idea to put on an AsyncTask for the following reason: Users will want to fire off a post (posting a photo, blog, tweet, or other data) and do something else, rather than waiting for a progress bar to clear. By using an AsyncTask, you're forcing them to wait around for the posting activity to finish.

- Last, be aware that there is some overhead for the system in setting up the AsyncTask. This is fine if you use a few of them, but it may start to slow down your main thread if you're firing off hundreds of them.

You might be curious as to exactly what you should use in these cases. I'm glad you are, because that's exactly what I'd like to show you next.

THE INTENTSERVICE

The IntentService is an excellent way to move large amounts of data around without relying on any specific activity or even application. The AsyncTask will always take over the main thread at least twice (with its pre- and post-execute methods), and it must be owned by an activity that is able to draw to the screen. The IntentService has no such restriction. To demonstrate, I'll show you how to download the same image, this time from the Intent Service rather than the AsyncTask.

DECLARING A SERVICE

Services are, essentially, classes that run in the background with no access to the screen. In order for the system to find your service when required, you'll need to declare it in your manifest, like so:

```xml
<?xml version="1.0" encoding="utf-8"?>
<manifest xmlns:android="http://schemas.android.com/apk/res/android"
     package="com.peachpit.Example"
     android:versionCode="1"
     android:versionName="1.0">
  <application
     android:name="MyApplication"
     android:icon="@drawable/icon"
     android:label="@string/app_name">
  <!--Rest of the application declarations go here -->
     <service android:name=".ImageIntentService"/>
  </application>
</manifest>
```

At a minimum, you'll need to have this simple declaration. It will then allow you to (as I showed you earlier with activities) explicitly launch your service. Here's the code to do exactly that:

```java
Intent i = new Intent(this, ImageIntentService.class);
i.putExtra("url", getIntent().getExtras().getString("url"));
startService(i);
```

At this point, the system will construct a new instance of your service, call its onCreate method, and then start firing data at the IntentService's handleIntent method. The intent service is specifically constructed to handle large amounts of work and processing off the main thread. The service's onCreate method *will* be called on the main thread, but subsequent calls to handleIntent are guaranteed by Android to be on a background thread (and this is where you should put your long-running code in any case).

Right, enough gabbing. Let me introduce you to the `ImageIntentService`. The first thing you'll need to pay attention to is the constructor:

```java
public class ImageIntentService extends IntentService{
    public ImageIntentService() {
        super("ImageIntentService");
    }
}
```

Notice that the constructor you must declare has no string as a parameter. The parent's constructor that you must call, however, must be passed a string. Your IDE will let you know that you must declare a constructor with a string, when in reality, you must declare it without one. This simple mistake can cause you several hours of intense face-to-desk debugging.

Once your service exists, and before anything else runs, the system will call your `onCreate` method. `onCreate` is an excellent time to run any housekeeping chores you'll need for the rest of the service's tasks (more on this when I show you the image downloader).

At last, the service can get down to doing some heavy lifting. Once it has been constructed and has had its `onCreate` method called, it will then receive a call to `handleIntent` for each time any other activity has called `startService`.

FETCHING IMAGES

The main difference between fetching images and fetching smaller, manageable data is that larger data sets (such as images or larger data retrievals) should not be bundled into a final broadcast intent (another major difference to the `AsyncTask`). Also, keep in mind that the service has no direct access to any activity, so it cannot ever access the screen on its own. Instead of modifying the screen, the `IntentService` will send a broadcast intent alerting all listeners that the image download is complete. Further, since the service cannot pass the actual image data along with that intent, you'll need to save the image to the SD card and include the path to that file in the final completion broadcast.

THE SETUP

Before you can use the external storage to cache the data, you'll need to create a cache folder for your application. A good place to check is when the `IntentService`'s `onCreate` method is called:

```java
public void onCreate(){
    super.onCreate();
    String tmpLocation = Environment.getExternalStorageDirectory().getPath() +
    → CACHE_FOLDER;
    cacheDir = new File(tmpLocation);
    if(!cacheDir.exists()){
        cacheDir.mkdirs();
    }
}
```

A NOTE ON FILE SYSTEMS

Relying on a file-system cache has an interesting twist with Android. On most phones, the internal storage space (used to install applications) is incredibly limited. You should not, under any circumstances, store large amounts of data anywhere on the local file system. Always save it to a location returned from getExternalStorageDirectory.

When you're saving files to the SD card, you must also be aware that nearly all pre-2.3 Android devices can have their SD cards removed (or mounted as a USB drive on the user's laptop). This means you'll need to gracefully handle the case where the SD card is missing. You'll also need to be able to forgo the file-system cache on the fly if you want your application to work correctly when the external drive is missing. There are a lot of details to be conscious of while implementing a persistent storage cache, but the benefits (offline access, faster start-up times, fewer app-halting loading dialogs) make it more than worth your effort.

Using Android's environment, you can determine the correct prefix for the external file system. Once you know the path to the eventual cache folder, you can then make sure the directory is in place. Yes, I know I told you to avoid file-system contact while on the main thread (and onCreate is called on the main thread), but checking and creating a directory is a small enough task that it should be all right. I'll leave this as an open question for you as you read through the rest of this chapter: Where might be a better place to put this code?

THE FETCH

Now that you've got a place to save images as you download them, it's time to implement the image fetcher. Here's the onHandleIntent method:

```java
protected void onHandleIntent(Intent intent) {
    String remoteUrl = intent.getExtras().getString("url");
    String location;
    String filename = remoteUrl.substring(
    remoteUrl.lastIndexOf(File.separator) + 1);
    File tmp = new File(
        cacheDir.getPath() + File.separator + filename);

    if (tmp.exists()) {
        location = tmp.getAbsolutePath();
        notifyFinished(location, remoteUrl);
        stopSelf();
        return;
    }
    try {
```

```
        URL url = new URL(remoteUrl);
        HttpURLConnection httpCon = (HttpURLConnection) url.openConnection();
        if (httpCon.getResponseCode() != 200) {
            throw new Exception("Failed to connect");
        }
        InputStream is = httpCon.getInputStream();
        FileOutputStream fos = new FileOutputStream(tmp);
        writeStream(is, fos);
        fos.flush();
        fos.close();
        is.close();
        location = tmp.getAbsolutePath();
        notifyFinished(location, remoteUrl);
    } catch (Exception e) {
        Log.e("Service", "Failed!", e);
    }
}
```

This is a lot of code. Fortunately, most of it is stuff you've seen before.

First, you retrieve the URL to be downloaded from the Extras bundle on the intent. Next, you determine a cache file name by taking the last part of the URL. Once you know what the file will eventually be called, you can check to see if it's already in the cache. If it is, you're finished, and you can notify the system that the image is available to load into the UI.

If the file isn't cached, you'll need to download it. By now you've seen the HttpUrl Connection code used to download an image at least once, so I won't bore you by covering it. Also, if you've written any Java code before, you probably know how to write an input stream to disk.

THE CLEANUP

At this point, you've created the cache file, retrieved it from the web, and written it to the aforementioned cache file. It's time to notify anyone who might be listening that the image is available. Here's the contents of the notifyFinished method that will tell the system both that the image is finished and where to get it.

```
public static final String TRANSACTION_DONE =
        "com.peachpit.TRANSACTION_DONE";
private void notifyFinished(String location, String remoteUrl){
    Intent i = new Intent(TRANSACTION_DONE);
    i.putExtra("location", location);
    i.putExtra("url", remoteUrl);
    ·ImageIntentService.this.sendBroadcast(i);
}
```

Anyone listening for the broadcast intent com.peachpit.TRANSACTION_DONE will be notified that an image download has finished. They will be able to pull both the URL (so they can tell if it was an image it actually requested) and the location of the cached file.

RENDERING THE DOWNLOAD

In order to interact with the downloading service, there are two steps you'll need to take. You'll need to start the service (with the URL you want it to fetch). Before it starts, however, you'll need to register a listener for the result broadcast. You can see these two steps in the following code:

```
public void onCreate(Bundle extras){
    super.onCreate(extras);
    setContentView(R.layout.image_layout);
    IntentFilter intentFilter = new IntentFilter();
    intentFilter.addAction(ImageIntentService.TRANSACTION_DONE);
    registerReceiver(imageReceiver, intentFilter);

    Intent i = new Intent(this, ImageIntentService.class);
    i.putExtra("url", getIntent().getExtras().getString("url"));
    startService(i);

    pd = ProgressDialog.show(this,
    "Fetching Image",
    "Go intent service go!");
}
```

This code registered a receiver (so you can take action once the download is finished), started the service, and, finally, showed a loading dialog box to the user.

Now take a look at what the imageReceiver class looks like:

```
private BroadcastReceiver imageReceiver = new BroadcastReceiver() {
    @Override
    public void onReceive(Context context, Intent intent) {
        String location = intent.getExtras().getString("location");
        if(TextUtils.isEmpty(location)){
            String failedString = "Failed to download image";
            Toast.makeText(context, failedString , Toast.LENGTH_LONG).show();
        }

        File imageFile = new File(location);
        if(!imageFile.exists()){
            pd.dismiss();
```

FIGURE 4.2 Developer option for enabling
strict mode

```
        String downloadFail = "Unable to Download file :-(";
        Toast.makeText(context, downloadFail, Toast.LENGTH_LONG);
        return;
    }

    Bitmap b = BitmapFactory.decodeFile(location);
    ImageView iv = (ImageView)findViewById(R.id.remote_image);
    iv.setImageBitmap(b);
    pd.dismiss();
  }
};
```

This is a custom extension of the BroadcastReceiver class. This is what you'll need to declare inside your activity to correctly process events from the IntentService. Right now, there are two problems with this code. See if you can recognize them.

First, you'll need to extract the file location from the intent. You do this by looking for the "location" extra. Once you've verified that this is indeed a valid file, you'll pass it over to the BitmapFactory, which will create the image for you. This bitmap can then be passed off to the ImageView for rendering.

Now, to the things done wrong (stop reading if you haven't found them yet—no cheating!). First, the code is not checking to see if the intent service is broadcasting a completion intent for exactly the image originally asked for (keep in mind that one service can service requests from any number of activities).

Second, the bitmap is loading from the SD card... on the main thread! Exactly one of the things I've been warning you NOT to do.

CHECKING YOUR WORK

Android, in later versions of the SDK tools, has provided a way to check if your application is breaking the rules and running slow tasks on the main thread. The easiest way to accomplish this is by enabling the setting in your developer options (**Figure 4.2**). If you want more fine-grained control of when it's enabled (or you're on a Gingerbread phone), you can, in any activity, call StrictMode.enableDefaults(). This will begin to throw warnings when the system spots main thread violations. StrictMode has many different configurations and settings, but enabling the defaults and cleaning up as many errors as you can will work wonders for the speed of your application.

WRAPPING UP

That about covers how to load data. Remember, loading from the SD card, network transactions, and longer processing tasks MUST be performed off the main thread, or your application, and users, will suffer. You can, as I've shown you in this chapter, use a simple thread, an AsyncTask, or an IntentService to retrieve and process your data. But remember, too, that any action modifying any view or object onscreen must be carried out on the main thread (or Android will throw angry exceptions at you).

Further, keep in mind that these three methods are only a few of many possible background data fetching patterns. Loaders, Workers, and ThreadPools are all other alternatives that might suit your application better than the examples I've given.

Follow the simple rules I've outlined here, and your app will be fast, it will be responsive to your users, it shouldn't crash (ha!), and it will avoid the dreaded App Not Responding notification of doom. Correct use and avoidance of the main thread is critical to producing a successful application.

If you're interested in building lists out of complex data from remote sources, the next chapter should give you exactly what you're looking for. I'll be showing you how to render a list of Twitter messages to a menu onscreen.

I'll leave you with a final challenge: Enable Android's strict mode and move the little file accesses I've left in this chapter's sample code off the main thread. It should be a good way to familiarize yourself with the process before you undertake it on your own.

CHAPTER 5

Adapters, List Views, and Lists

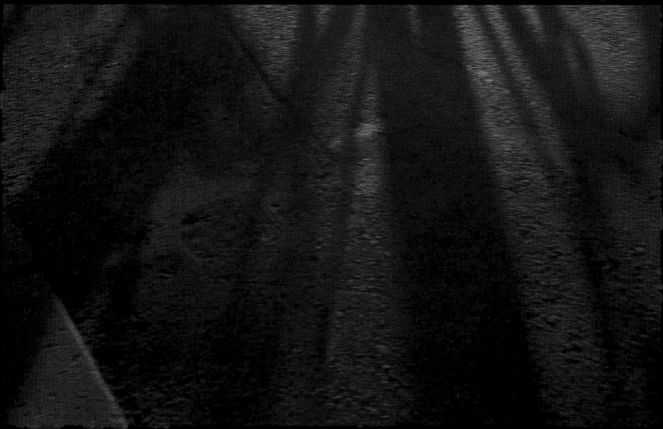

Lists, in Android, are one of the most often-used tools to show data to users. From the entry menu of a game to a dynamic list of Facebook statuses or Twitter messages, lists are everywhere. Android's system for dealing with them, while complicated at first, becomes much easier once you begin using it. In this chapter, I'll run the gamut from simple, static main-menu lists to the dynamic, remote-data-backed custom list elements of a Reddit feed (the social news and entertainment website). Along the way, I'll expose you to the inner workings of one of Android's most often-used and complex UI views.

TWO PIECES TO EACH LIST

To display lists of ordered data with Android, there are two major components you'll need to deal with.

LISTVIEW

First, you'll need a ListView in which to display your content. This is the view whose job it is to display the information. It can be added to any screen layout, or you can use Android's ListActivity or ListFragment to handle some of the organization for you. If your screen is primarily designed to show a collection of data to the user in list form, I highly suggest you use ListActivity and its cousin ListFragment.

ADAPTER

The second major class you'll need to deal with is the Adapter. This is the object that will feed the individual views, a little bit at a time, to the ListView. It's also responsible for filling and configuring the individual rows to be populated in the ListView. There are as many Adapter subclasses as drops of water in the ocean (all right, perhaps slightly fewer), and they cover the range of data types—from static string lists (ArrayAdapters) to the more dynamic lists (CursorAdapters). You can extend your own adapter (which I'll show you in the second half of this chapter). For now, let me show you how to create a simple main menu with a ListView.

As always, you can either follow along with the sample code I've posted at Peachpit.com/androiddevelopanddesign or open your IDE and do the tasks I've outlined.

A MAIN MENU

Main menus can take any number of forms. From games to music apps, they provide a top-level navigation for the app as a whole.

They are also, as a happy side effect, a great way to introduce you to how lists work. I'll be creating an array of strings for the resource manager, feeding it to an array adapter, and plugging that array adapter into the list view contained by a list activity. Got all that? There are a lot of moving parts to collect when dealing with lists, so I'll take it slowly and step by step.

CREATING THE MENU DATA

A menu must have something to display, so you need to create a list of strings to be displayed. Remember the chapter where you learned that all displayed string constants *should* go into the res/values/strings.xml file? String arrays, coincidentally, go into the same file, but with a slightly different syntax. I've added the following to my res/values/strings.xml file:

```xml
<?xml version="1.0" encoding="utf-8"?>
<resources>
    <!--The rest of the app's strings here-->
    <string name="app_name">List Example</string>
    <string name="main_menu">Main Menu</string>
    <string-array name="menu_entries">
        <item>Menu Item One</item>
        <item>Menu Item Two</item>
        <item>Menu Item Three</item>
        <item>Menu Item Four</item>
        <item>Menu Item Five</item>
        <item>Menu Item Six</item>
        <item>Menu Item Seven</item>
    </string-array>

</resources>
```

Instead of defining each constant inside a string tag, this time you'll declare a string array with a name, and then each element within it can be defined inside an item tag. Now that you have data, it's time to create an activity in which to house it.

CREATING A LISTACTIVITY

Now you need a place to display your items. You'll create an instance of ListActivity in which to display your recently created list.

Every screen must have an activity, and list screens are no exception. In this case, Android provides you a helper class that was built specifically to make list screens easier. It's called the ListActivity, and it behaves exactly like an activity does except that it has a few extra methods to make life easier. If you're coding along with the chapter, you'll need to create a new project. Take the main activity you'd normally have, and modify it to look like the following listing:

```java
package com.peachpit.lists;
import android.app.ListActivity;
import android.os.Bundle;
public class MainMenuActivity extends ListActivity{
    public void onCreate(Bundle bundle){
        super.onCreate(bundle);
        setContentView(R.layout.list_activity);
    }
}
```

This code will not, however, compile at the moment, because I haven't yet defined what R.layout.list_activity looks like. Guess what you're going to do next?

DEFINING A LAYOUT FOR YOUR LISTACTIVITY

You will need to create an XML layout file for your list. Again, this is similar to other layout tasks you've done, with one notable exception: You need to define a ListView with the special ID android:id/list. This is what tells the system which list view is the main list view your new ListActivity will interact with. I've also added a TextView to the layout as a large title. My XML file looks like the following:

```
<?xml version="1.0" encoding="utf-8"?>
<LinearLayout xmlns:android="http://schemas.android.com/apk/res/android"
    android:layout_width="match_parent"
    android:layout_height="match_parent"
    android:orientation="vertical">
    <TextView
        android:layout_width="match_parent"
        android:layout_height="0dp"
        android:layout_weight="1"
        android:gravity="center"
        android:text="@string/main_menu"
        android:gravity="center"
        android:textSize="40sp" />
    <ListView
        android:id="@android:id/list"
        android:layout_width="match_parent"
        android:layout_height="0dp"
        android:layout_weight="1"
        android:gravity="center" />
</LinearLayout>
```

> **TIP:** Special IDs: You only need to call the android:id/list ListView if you're using the built-in convenience methods of ListActivity. If you're using a regular activity, you can use any ID you want. This special ID is what connects the ListActivity to the single ListView with which it is going to interact.

This XML layout code should look familiar to you, given what you've read in previous chapters. It's simply splitting the screen space between the title main menu and the list of sub-screens. You can also see the special Android list ID that is needed to tell the ListActivity which view it should interact with.

MAKING A MENU LIST ITEM

Now you'll create a layout XML file for the individual list element.

You'll need to declare a separate layout object to define how each element will look in the list. I'm using a very simple version of the ArrayAdapter, so at this point, the layout XML file *must* contain only a single text view. We'll get into more-complex menu items later in the chapter.

Next, you'll need to create a new file, containing a single text view, in the /res/layout/ folder. Here's what /res/layout/list_element.xml looks like in my project:

```xml
<?xml version="1.0" encoding="utf-8"?>
<TextView xmlns:android="http://schemas.android.com/apk/res/android"
    android:layout_width="match_parent"
    android:gravity="center"
    android:layout_height="wrap_content"
    android:gravity="center"
    android:textSize="20sp"
    android:padding="15dp" />
```

You don't actually need to supply an ID for this text view, because you'll be referencing it in its capacity as a layout object (R.layout.list_element, in this case). Setting the gravity to center tells the view that you want the text to lie in the center of the extra available space. Setting the padding to 15dp will also give the views a little bit of extra space, so people with hands like mine can hit the correct one.

Now that I've declared what I want the list elements to look like, I can go about adding them to the ListView itself.

CREATING AND POPULATING THE ARRAYADAPTER

Create and configure an ArrayAdapter. The ArrayAdapter will communicate your data to the ListView. It will also inflate however many copies of the list_element layout are needed to keep the ListView full of data. As a last step, here's what you'll need to add to the MainMenuActivity's onCreate method:

```
public void onCreate(Bundle bundle){
    super.onCreate(bundle);
    setContentView(R.layout.list_activity);
    ArrayAdapter<String> adapter = ArrayAdapter.createFromResource(this,
    R.array.menu_entries, R.layout.list_element);
    setListAdapter(adapter);
}
```

Because the ListView has the special @android:id/list system ID, the ListActivity knows where to find the ListView. As a result, you'll only have to create the adapter and hand it over to the ListActivity. The ListActivity will make sure that it's correctly plugged into the ListView and that everything is drawn correctly.

To create the ArrayAdapter, I specify the array of strings I defined in the section "Creating the Menu Data" as well as the list_element layout I created in "Making a Menu List Item." Assuming that all your components are hooked up correctly, the resulting screen will look something like **Figure 5.1**.

Do a little dance—you've now got a functional (albeit very simple) list! Have a cup of coffee, sip of wine, or dog treat. Whatever you do to reward yourself for a job well done, do it now. I'll be here when you get back.

REACTING TO CLICK EVENTS

Your code will need to listen for item clicks.

What's the point of having a menu if you can't tell when items have been selected? Right, there isn't one. Let me show you the final piece to my basic list menu example. Add the following method to your MainMenuActivity.java file:

```
@Override
public void onListItemClick(ListView listView, View clickedView,
        int position, long id) {
    super.onListItemClick(listView clickedView, position, id);
    TextView tv = (TextView) clickedView;
    String clickText = "List Item " + tv.getText() + " was clicked!";
    Toast.makeText(getBaseContext(), clickText, Toast.LENGTH_SHORT).show();
}
```

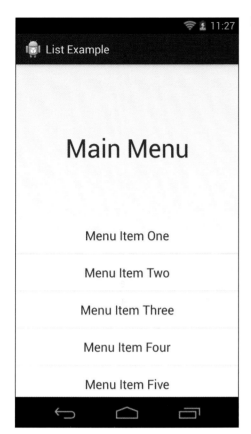

FIGURE 5.1 A very basic main menu

The ListActivity will call this method (if you've defined it) every time an element in the list view is clicked. For more-complicated lists, you may want to use the ID—for example, if you are fetching your list contents from an SQLite database. For this simple demo, I've just popped up a little dialog showing the text of the item that was pressed. If you're implementing your own basic main menu, I suggest you use the position of the clicked item to start an activity, service, or other action. You can see an example of this if you look at the associated source code.

That's the most basic list view I could possibly show you. Now, I'll take you in the opposite direction and show you what a custom list backed by a remote data source looks like.

COMPLEX LIST VIEWS

While building a main menu is great and all, there are much more complicated uses to which you can put the Adapter and `ListView` combination. In fact, I'm going to show you an example that gets complicated in two ways. First, the data source is going to be from a remote URL (a Reddit feed). Second, I'm going to add a second text view to the list (you could, if you want to, add any number of items to it).

THE 1000-FOOT VIEW

All right, here's the game plan. First, you'll need an `AsyncTask` to retrieve the feed from Reddit's API. Once you have the data, you'll need to parse it into JSON (JavaScript Object Notation) objects and feed that data into a custom adapter. Since this is a book on Android development and not JSON development, I'm going to leverage Google's JSON parser, GSON. If you want to see how it works, the project is open source, but for the sake of this demo, you shouldn't need to worry about it. Last, you'll need to create that custom adapter and the specific `ListView` layout to hold the two pieces of text information. With those things in hand, you can create the custom layout object.

In the end, you'll have a list of the most recently popular *subreddits* (nomenclature for groupings of similar content or interests) on Reddit, as well as an indicator of whether the subreddit accepts links, self-posts, or anything. These indicators will change color and letter for each respective type. This is by no means the most complex list you could build using these tools, but it is a great way to show you how to make your own complex custom list views.

CREATING THE MAIN LAYOUT VIEW

This step is very similar to the "Defining a Layout for Your ListActivity" section. You'll need an XML layout containing a `ListView` with the `android:id/list` ID. In this case, however, because the data isn't available when the activity launches, you'll want the `ListView` to start out hidden. Here's what my project's XML layout looks like. (Don't be alarmed by all the styling in this example; might as well make it look pretty, right?)

```
<LinearLayout xmlns:android="http://schemas.android.com/apk/res/android"
    android:layout_width="match_parent"
    android:layout_height="match_parent"
    android:orientation="vertical">

    <TextView
        android:layout_width="match_parent"
        android:layout_height="wrap_content"
        android:background="#888888"
        android:fontFamily="sans-serif-light"
```

```
        android:gravity="center"
        android:padding="10dp"
        android:text="Popular on Reddit"
        android:textColor="#FFFFFF"
        android:textSize="24sp"
        android:textStyle="bold" />

    <RelativeLayout
        android:layout_width="match_parent"
        android:layout_height="match_parent">

        <ProgressBar
            android:id="@+id/empty_view"
            android:layout_width="wrap_content"
            android:layout_height="wrap_content"
            android:layout_centerInParent="true"
            android:indeterminate="true"
            android:text="Loading..."/>

        <ListView
            android:id="@android:id/list"
            android:layout_width="match_parent"
            android:layout_height="match_parent"
            android:paddingLeft="10dp"
            android:paddingRight="10dp"/>
    </RelativeLayout>
</LinearLayout>
```

CREATING THE LISTACTIVITY

Again, you're going to need a new ListActivity. Since you're already good at getting them started, I'll just skip to showing you what my onCreate method looks like:

```
RedditAsyncTask mTask;
@Override
protected void onCreate(Bundle savedInstanceState) {
    super.onCreate(savedInstanceState);
    setContentView(R.layout.activity_main);
```

```
// What the user will see when the list is loading
ProgressBar progress = (ProgressBar) findViewById(R.id.empty_view);
getListView().setEmptyView(progress);

mTask = new RedditAsyncTask();
mTask.execute("http://www.reddit.com/subreddits/popular.json");
}
```

NOTE: If the Reddit URL in the earlier code listing isn't working, I've stashed a backup copy of the data at http://wanderingoak.net/reddit_backup.json. If Reddit changes their API, you can always run the sample code against that URL.

The most important thing here is that we are executing the RedditAsyncTask, which kicks off the thread and starts the whole network process. Without execute(...), the task won't actually run.

You'll have noticed, if you were watching closely, that I created a private data member to contain the Reddit-fetching task. You astute readers might be wondering why I chose to stash it aside that way. The answer is that because this task isn't happening on the main thread, I need to be able to cancel it should the user close down the activity before the task finishes. To do this, the onStop method will need to be able to call the Reddit-fetching AsyncTask, making it a private data member.

GETTING REDDIT DATA

My first task, at least when it comes to doing work, is to load the stream of popular subreddits. You should, thanks to the previous chapter, be very familiar with the ins and outs of fetching network data, so a lot of this should seem straightforward. This is where that JSON parsing we talked about earlier comes into play. If you're having a hard time grasping how GSON works, don't worry about it! The more you work with it, the more sense it starts to make.

Without further preamble, here's what my RedditAsyncTask looks like:

```
private class RedditAsyncTask extends
    AsyncTask<String, Integer, PopularSubreddit[]> {
    @Override
    protected PopularSubreddit[] doInBackground(String... params) {
        try {

            String url = params[0];
            HttpClient httpClient = new DefaultHttpClient();
            HttpGet post = new HttpGet(url);
            HttpResponse rp = httpClient.execute(post);
```

```java
    if (rp.getStatusLine().getStatusCode() == HttpStatus.SC_OK) {

        String response = EntityUtils.toString(rp.getEntity());
        JsonParser parser = new JsonParser();
        // Turn response into a JsonObject
        JsonObject element = parser.parse(response).getAsJsonObject();
        // Get the children posts out of the JsonObject
        JsonElement jsonSubreddits =
            element.get("data").getAsJsonObject().get("children");
        Gson gson = new Gson();
        // Gson magically turns Json into the class you want!
        PopularSubreddit[] subreddits = gson.fromJson(jsonSubreddits,
            PopularSubreddit[].class);

        return subreddits;
    } else {
        return null;
    }
} catch (Exception e) {
    e.printStackTrace();
    return null;
}


@Override
protected void onPostExecute(PopularSubreddit[] subreddits) {
    if (subreddits!= null) {
```

```
        RedditAdapter adapter =
            new RedditAdapter(getBaseContext(),subreddits);
        setListAdapter(adapter);
    }
  }
}
```

Here are the general steps for fetching the data:

1. Fetch the data, and using your preferred JSON parsing method, turn the response into usable Java objects.

2. Once you're back on the main thread inside the onPostExecute method, create a new adapter with all the subreddits that you have parsed, and set the adapter onto the list. Voilà! You're done!

NOTE: Any changes to the Adapter's data must take place on the main thread. Modifying the Adapter data counts as changing the UI, as far as Android is concerned. As always, all changes to the user interface must be carried out on the main thread. Keep this is mind as you create your own adapter, especially if you're fetching data from the network off the main thread.

MAKING A CUSTOM ADAPTER

All right, now comes the really interesting part. You need to create a custom Adapter to feed rows into the ListView.

Custom Adapters have four methods you are required to override, all of which allow the ListView to acquire information about your data set.

- getCount() returns the number of rows currently in the set of information.

- getItem(int position) returns an object corresponding to a particular row position.

- getItemId(int position) returns the ID that corresponds to the item at a specific position. This is often used with Adapters that focus on Cursors (Android's SQLite interfaces).

- getView(int position, View convertView, ViewGroup parent) is where most of the Adapter's work will take place. The ListView, in making this call, is essentially asking for the view at position. You must, in this method, return a correctly configured view for the data at position. More on exactly how this works in a minute.

As you can see by the get prefix on all the required methods, all that Android Adapters do is provide row content information to the ListView. The ListView, it would seem, is one very needy girlfriend (or boyfriend... I'm not sure how to assign gender to Android UI interfaces).

Let me show you the example before I talk about any more theory. Since earlier I parsed out all the popular subreddits into an array, I'm going to use this array as the data backing our adapter. This class is declared as a separate class in the same package as your activity.

```java
public class RedditAdapter extends BaseAdapter {

    PopularSubreddit[] mSubreddits;
    Context mContext;

    public RedditAdapter(Context context, PopularSubreddit[] subreddits) {
        mContext = context;
        mSubreddits = subreddits;
    }

    @Override
    public int getCount() {
        if (mSubreddits == null) {
            return 0;
        } else {
            return mSubreddits.length;
        }
    }

    @Override
    public PopularSubreddit getItem(int position) {
        if (mSubreddits == null != position >= 0 &&
            position < mSubreddits.length) {
            return subreddits[position];
        } else {
            return null;
        }
    }

    @Override
    public long getItemId(int position) {
        return position;
    }
}
```

This code, for the most part, provides functions access to the `PopularSubreddit` data that is initialized in the constructor. It handles getting an item from a position. If there is no data (maybe it was cleared), then the `Adapter` simply reports that there's nothing to see. This class extends from `BaseAdapter` because it contains all the baseline methods that I need to build my custom adapter.

BUILDING THE LISTVIEWS

At last you've come to the part where you get to build and return the individual custom list view elements. Here's the code to do exactly that:

```java
@Override
public View getView(int position, View convertView, ViewGroup parent) {

    PopularSubreddit subreddit = getItem(position);
    View view;

    //Reduce, Reuse, Recycle!
    if (convertView == null) {
        view = LayoutInflater.from(mContext).
            inflate(R.layout.list_item_reddit_popular, parent, false);

    } else {
        view = convertView;
    }

    TextView tv = (TextView) view.findViewById(R.id.header_text);
    String title = subreddit.data.title;
    tv.setText(title.toUpperCase());

    tv = (TextView) view.findViewById(R.id.sub_text);
    tv.setText(subreddit.data.public_description);

    TextView submissionTypeView = (TextView)
        view.findViewById(R.id.submission_view);
    if ("link".equals(subreddit.data.submission_type)) {
        submissionTypeView.setText("L");
        submissionTypeView.setBackgroundColor(0x77FF0000);
```

```
    } else if ("self".equals(subreddit.data.submission_type)) {
        submissionTypeView.setText("S");
        submissionTypeView.setBackgroundColor(0x7700FF00);

    } else if ("any".equals(subreddit.data.submission_type)) {
        submissionTypeView.setText("A");
        submissionTypeView.setBackgroundColor(0x770000FF);

    } else {
        submissionTypeView.setText("?");
        submissionTypeView.setBackgroundColor(0x77222222);
    }

    return view;
}
```

There are a couple of key points to consider in the getView code listing.

First, you need to figure out if the view can be recycled. If it can, you'll reset *all* the visible values for it; otherwise, you'll inflate a new row—by using the LayoutInflater—and configure it (more on how and why this works soon).

Second, you'll get the title and description text from the Subreddit object and set them onto their respective TextViews.

Lastly, you will change the background color and text label of the submission type view to indicate to the user what kind of submissions this subreddit accepts. You might have noticed that I haven't showed you what list_item_reddit_popular.xml looks like. That is the view layout I'm creating (by calling the inflate method and passing in the layout).

THE CUSTOM LAYOUT VIEW

This layout has three TextViews in it, with the IDs submission_view, header_text, and sub_text. These can be found in res/layout/list_item_reddit_popular:

```
<LinearLayout xmlns:android="http://schemas.android.com/apk/res/android"
    android:layout_width="match_parent"
    android:layout_height="wrap_content"
    android:padding="10dp"
    android:orientation="vertical">
```

```
<LinearLayout
    android:layout_width="match_parent"
    android:layout_height="wrap_content"
    android:orientation="horizontal">

    <TextView
        android:id="@+id/accepted_submissions_view"
        android:layout_width="16dp"
        android:layout_height="16dp"
        android:fontFamily="sans-serif-condensed"
        android:gravity="center"
        android:layout_gravity="center_vertical"
        android:layout_marginRight="10dp"
        android:textSize="8sp" />

    <TextView
        android:id="@+id/header_text"
        android:layout_width="wrap_content"
        android:layout_height="wrap_content"
        android:layout_gravity="center_vertical"
        android:fontFamily="sans-serif-condensed"
        android:textSize="18sp"
        android:textColor="#444444" />
</LinearLayout>

<TextView
    android:id="@+id/sub_text"
    android:layout_width="wrap_content"
    android:layout_height="wrap_content"
    android:maxLines="3"
    android:textColor="#666666" />
</LinearLayout>
```

With this layout, you now have all the moving pieces you need to download, parse, and display the most popular subreddits feed. **Figure 5.2**, at last, is what the popular subreddit viewer looks like in `ListView` form.

FIGURE 5.2 The list of the most popular subreddits!

HOW DO THESE OBJECTS INTERACT?

To understand how the ListView interacts with the Adapter, there are a few constraints you must understand. First, lists could scroll on to infinity, at least from the point of view of the device. Yet, as you might have guessed, the phone has a limited amount of memory. This means that not every single list item can have its own entry in the list, because the device would quickly run out of space. Further, if the ListView had to lay out every single row right up front, it could be bogged down for an unacceptable amount of time.

What Android does to solve these problems is to recycle list element rows. The process looks a little bit like this:

1. Android goes through the entire list, asking each row how large it would like to be (this is so it knows how large to draw the scroll indicator).

2. Once it knows roughly how big the entire ListView will be, it then requests views for the first screen, plus a buffer (so it won't have to stop and get more when the user starts scrolling). Your adapter will have to create, configure, and return those views as the ListView calls getView over and over again.

3. As the user scrolls down and rows fall off the top of the list, Android will return them to you when it calls getView. Effectively, it's asking you to reuse a previous view by passing in the convertView object to you.

NOTE: Any asynchronous task, such as loading an icon from disk or loading a user's profile icon, must check that the ListView hasn't recycled the view while it's been downloading or loading the image data. If the row is still showing the same data when the task finishes, it's safe to update the row; otherwise, it needs to cache or chuck the data.

MORE THAN ONE LIST ITEM TYPE

Sometimes, you will be displaying list contents that have more than one view type. For example, you might be displaying content that has images interspersed with text. While you could certainly create a row item that contains all the items and hide or show the relevant parts, it might make more sense to have separate view types to display them.

```
public class MultiTypeAdapter extends BaseAdapter{
    private static final int TYPE_TEXT = 0;
    private static final int TYPE_IMAGE = 1;

    @Override
    public int getViewTypeCount() {
        return 2;
    }

    @Override
    public int getItemViewType(int position) {
        if (getItem() instance String) {
            return TYPE_TEXT;
        } else {
            return TYPE_IMAGE;
        }
    }
}
```

By returning 2 from getViewTypeCount(), we are letting the adapter know that there are two different views we are recycling, so please hold on to both of them. Then, when the system tries to determine which recycled view to give you, it calls getItemViewType() and asks you to tell it what type of view should be used for the data at the given position. There is no limit to how many different view types you can have in an adapter, but keep in mind that the more you have, the more it will keep in memory.

WRAPPING UP

This chapter covered the basics of both simple and custom ListViews and Adapters. I showed you how to create a simple main menu, and I walked you through a simple example of building a custom Adapter to handle a more complex ListView. You now have a grasp of the basics.

Lists are still one of the cornerstones of mobile development. I advise you, however, to make as few boring, graphically flat lists as you possibly can. While these examples are great for showing you how to build lists of your own, they are by no means shining examples of solid interface design. You can, and very much should, make lists when needed, but dress them up as much as you can without affecting performance.

If you're hungering for more, I highly suggest reading through Android's implementation of ListActivity.java or ListFragment.java. Because Android is open source, you can get all the code that makes up its SDK for free! Head over to http://source.android.com for more information.

Lastly, I wrote more code for this chapter than I had space to explain here. I recommend checking out the sample code associated with this chapter (at Peachpit.com/androiddevelopanddesign) to learn more about launching a screen as the result of a menu click and about how to build a similar main menu screen using a ListFragment.

CHAPTER 6

Background Services

Services are one of the most important, and most often under-utilized, components of the Android platform. They are essential for accomplishing any task whose data or relevance can span more than one activity. They are like activities in that they have a lifecycle (albeit a much simpler one), but they do not have the activity's ability to draw to the screen. In practice, services break down into two major use cases: the listener and the task. Listeners are services that hang out in the background, waiting for something to happen that prompts them to take action. Task services are akin to the photo downloader that we covered before, so in this chapter I'll focus on listening services.

WHAT IS A SERVICE?

A Service is, at its most basic level, a class with a simple runtime lifecycle and no access to the screen. You had some contact with the `IntentService` back in Chapter 4 when I showed you how to retrieve an image with it, but I now have the chance to help you really dig into this simple yet powerful component.

Keep in mind that while the service might be important to *you*, it is not more important to Android than the smooth running of the overall device. This means that at any point the system may shut down your service if it determines that it's been running too long, that it's been consuming too many resources, or that it's the third Friday of the month and there's a full moon. There is a way to tell the system not to kill you off, and I'll show what that looks like in just a second.

THE SERVICE LIFECYCLE

A service is, essentially, a singleton. Any component in your application may call `startService` with an intent that specifies the service they want to get running. If the service isn't running, Android will initialize a new one; otherwise, it will just notify the existing one that a new start command has been issued. Here's a brief rundown of the service's lifecycle.

- `onCreate` is called on the main thread when the service is started up. It's a good time to initialize any data you're going to rely on throughout the run of the service.
- `onStartCommand` will be called every time an activity (or any other component) calls `startService`. The intent passed into `startService` will be handed off to your `onStartCommand` call.
- `onBind` is your chance to return, to the caller, an interface object that allows direct method calls on the service. The binder, however, is optional and only really needed for a heavy level of communication with your service. This results in a different method of interaction than calling `Context.startService`. Like `startService`, `bindService` takes an intent and will start up the service if it's not already running. If absolutely none of what you just read makes sense, that's fine; it'll make much more sense to you by the end of the chapter.

At this point in the lifecycle, your service is happily running along. Music can be played, data can be acquired (remember the main thread!), and recordings can be made and crunched for voice commands.

KEEPING YOUR SERVICE RUNNING

The startForeground method is your chance to strike a clever deal with Android. The system agrees that after you call this method and until you call stopForeground, it will not kill off your service. In exchange, you must provide an icon and view to be shown to the user in the top bar by handing it a Notification object. This contract allows long-running, essential, and intensive services (such as music playback or photo uploading) to run without fear of extermination. At the same time, the user is aware of why their phone might be a little sluggish.

SHUT IT DOWN!

At some point, the party will end and it'll be time to clean up. This can happen because your service called stopSelf or because another component called Context.stopService. Here's the teardown portion of the lifecycle:

- onDestroy is your chance to cancel any running tasks and put away any resource you've taken on (for example, media or network tasks). This is also your chance to unregister any BroadcastReceivers or ContentObservers that you've set up to watch for new media.

    If you were expecting a many-step shutdown process, I'm afraid you're going to be disappointed. Because services have no notion of being on top of the screen, there is no need to pause, resume, or do any of the other complex interactions that activities must support.

COMMUNICATION

There are two main ways to communicate with a service: intent broadcasts and binder interfaces. I'm going to show you examples of both and, along the way, let you see two practical tasks for a service. There are, in fact, many more ways you can communicate with your services, but in my experience, these are the two most useful. As always, check the documentation if neither of these approaches feels quite right for you.

INTENT-BASED COMMUNICATION

Imagine two workers in different rooms who can communicate with each other only by email. These emails can contain attachments and other pieces of data. The two workers must get through their day using only this one method of communication. As you might imagine, this can be an efficient and functional way to get a multitude of things done, as long as they don't have to say too much to each other.

This is, in a sense, exactly what *intent-based communication* with services would look like translated to real life. The service is started with an Intent. When it completes its task, or something that it's waiting for occurs, it sends a broadcast intent alerting anyone listening that a particular task is finished. You saw one example of this in Chapter 4 when downloading images using an intent service. Let me show you one more.

The following example is one of the best examples of intent-based communication that I can give you in this printed form. I'll create all the pieces required for a new service that runs, with a notification, in the foreground. I use Android's ContentProvider to listen for and acquire the location of new photographs as they are taken. This code will alert you when any new picture is snapped, regardless of the application used to do it. What you do with the photograph, I'll leave to your boundless imagination.

AUTO IMAGE UPLOADING

One of my favorite features of the Google+ Android app is its ability to upload photos automatically in the background. It turns out that with a ContentProvider, a Service, and a ContentObserver, you can do this quite easily in your own app. My sample service will launch, place itself in the foreground, and trigger a broadcast intent whenever a new photo is taken. You could, in your own code, upload the image or take any number of other actions. Using this technique would involve the following general steps.

1. Declare the service.
2. Get yourself a service.
3. Start the service.
4. Spin up the service.
5. Go to the foreground.
6. Observe when content changes.

Let's get started.

DECLARING THE SERVICE

You must tell Android where to find the service.

Each service, as you know, must be declared in the manifest. You can add an intent filter for it to respond to (if you want applications other than your own to be able to start it). For my example, this isn't necessary, but it might be something you need to take advantage of later. Here's the single line you'll need to place in your manifest:

```
<service android:name="PhotoListenerService"/>
```

GETTING YOURSELF A SERVICE

Now create the class that extends the service.

```
public class PhotoListenerService extends Service {
   @Override
   public IBinder onBind(Intent intent) {
      return null;
   }
}
```

Since onBind is a required method for the Service class, it has to be in my class or it won't compile. Now that you've got a service, let's look at how to actually start it.

STARTING THE SERVICE

Start the service from your activity. When I created the project, I got a default activity (I named mine, quite originally, ServiceExampleActivity) and a main.xml view.

1. Modify that view to contain Start and Stop buttons, like so:

```
<?xml version="1.0" encoding="utf-8"?>
<LinearLayout xmlns:android="http://schemas.android.com/apk/res/android"
   android:layout_width="match_parent"
   android:layout_height="match_parent"
   android:orientation="vertical"
   android:padding="15dp" >

   <Button
      android:id="@+id/start_service"
      android:layout_width="match_parent"
      android:layout_height="wrap_content"
      android:gravity="center"
      android:padding="15dp"
      android:text="Start service" />

   <Button
      android:id="@+id/stop_service"
      android:layout_width="match_parent"
      android:layout_height="wrap_content"
      android:gravity="center"
      android:padding="15dp"
      android:text="Stop service" />
</LinearLayout>
```

The buttons are a simple way to put some clickable text on the screen.

2. With these in place, you can now write code to start and stop the photo listening service. Here's what the updated ServiceExampleActivity now looks like:

```
public class ServiceExampleActivity extends Activity
        implements OnClickListener{
  /** Called when the activity is first created. */
  @Override
  public void onCreate(Bundle savedInstanceState) {
      super.onCreate(savedInstanceState);
      setContentView(R.layout.main);
      Button btn = (Button) findViewById(R.id.start_service);
      btn.setOnClickListener(this);
      btn = (Button) findViewById(R.id.stop_service);
      btn.setOnClickListener(this);
  }
}
```

Nothing earth-shattering in this listing. I'm retrieving references to the views once they've been built. I set my class to implement the OnClickListener interface, which allows me to set the activity itself as the click listener for the two buttons. The above code will not compile until you implement View.onClick.

3. Implement the onClick method:

```
@Override
public void onClick(View v) {
    Intent serviceIntent = new Intent(
        getApplicationContext(), PhotoListenerService.class);
    if(v.getId() == R.id.start_service){
        startService(serviceIntent);

    } else if(v.getId() == R.id.stop_service){
        stopService(serviceIntent);
    }
}
```

This, again, is pretty simple. The buttons, when clicked, will call this onClick method. Depending on the view that actually got the click, I'll either start or stop the service.

SPINNING UP THE SERVICE

Right now, if you were to run the code as it stands, you'd press the button, the service would start, and... nothing whatsoever would happen. Let me show you how to change that.

I want to be notified by the system every time someone takes a picture with the device's camera. To do this, you'll have to register an observer with Android's media

ContentProvider. Switching back to the `PhotoListenerService.java` file, register for media notifications in the service's onCreate method:

```java
@Override
public void onCreate(){
    super.onCreate();
    getContentResolver().registerContentObserver(
        MediaStore.Images.Media.EXTERNAL_CONTENT_URI,
        true, mContentObserver);
}
```

> **TIP:** `MediaStore.Images.Media.EXTERNAL_CONTENT_URI` is an Android constant that is present on all distributions of Android. It's a URI pointing to the default location where images are stored. There are similar URIs for audio (`Audio.Media.EXTERNAL_CONTENT_URI`) and video (`MediaStore.Video.Media.EXTERNAL_CONTENT_URI`).

To register a content observer, I'll need to provide a uniform resource identifier (URI). In this case, I'll use the constant URI for all photos saved on the external SD card. This constant is declared in the `MediaStore`. The second parameter is me telling Android that I'd like to know when children of that URI are modified. I set it to true because I'll want to know when any of the descendants of the image URI are modified, added, or deleted (`false` means only notify me when the exact URI is matched). Last, I pass in my observer. This is the object whose onChange method will be called whenever the `ContentProvider` is updated. It will register for media updates, but there's still one more method you'll need to define.

GOING TO THE FOREGROUND

Bringing your service into the foreground protects it from being killed by Android when resources are low.

Implement the onStartCommand method of your service as follows.

```java
public int onStartCommand(Intent intent, int flags, int startId) {
    super.onStartCommand(intent, flags, startId);
    lastUpdateTime = System.currentTimeMillis();

    Notification notification = buildSimpleNotification();
    startForeground(1, notification);

    return Service.START_STICKY;
}
```

I'm going to record when the service started (more on why that's important in just a second). Last, I return `Service.START_STICKY`, which tells the system that, should the service be terminated for memory or performance reasons, I'd like to have it started back up.

I need to write a function to build the notification and handle what happens when you click it. buildSimpleNotification() is our function, and it is using a helper class named NotificationBuilder to make building notifications quick and easy.

```
private Notification buildSimpleNotification() {

    NotificationCompat.Builder builder = new
        NotificationCompat.Builder(this);
    builder.setSmallIcon(R.drawable.icon);
    builder.setContentTitle("Photos uploading");
    builder.setContentText("Service Is uploading all your photos");
    builder.setTicker("Service started");

    Intent clickIntent = new Intent(getApplicationContext(),
        ServiceExampleActivity.class);
        PendingIntent pendingIntent = PendingIntent.getActivity(
        getApplicationContext(), 0, clickIntent, 0);
    builder.setContentIntent(pendingIntent);

    return builder.build();
}
```

Thanks to the wonders of line wrapping, this code is a little tricky to read. Essentially, in order to build the notification allowing you to go into foreground mode, you need at the very least a Notification object, which has an intent that fires when the user clicks the pull-down notification. Let me break it down a little more.

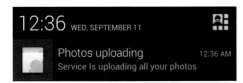

FIGURE 6.1 The notification pull-down in action!

Start by creating a `Notification` object using `NotificationCompat.Builder`, which requires five things to look and behave properly:

- A small icon resource, to be constantly displayed along the top of the notification bar
- A string for the ticker text, to be briefly flashed along the top bar when the notification appears
- A title of what to display in the notification
- A description of what is happening in the notification
- A `PendingIntent` holding the action of what to do when the notification is clicked

Although the last four settings are nice to have, the only required one for a valid notification is the small icon. Without it, your notification will fail to show.

The `PendingIntent` is the intent that is to be fired when the user presses the notification row seen in **Figure 6.1**. A `PendingIntent` is really just an intent and an instruction about what to do with it when the time comes. In this case, I want to launch the activity with the Start and Stop buttons. You'll set the `PendingIntent`, as I did, to be the notification's `contentIntent`.

With the fully built notification in hand, you can now call `startForeground` and hand it the notification. We're calling `startForeground(1, notification)`, where 1 is a constant for representing this notification. The number can be anything, as long as it doesn't change and as long as it's not 0.

You've now met your half of the contract: You've told the user who you are and why you're running. The system will now allow you to run uninterrupted until such time as the user disables the service by pressing the activity's Stop button. It's time to start listening for when the content changes.

OBSERVING WHEN CONTENT CHANGES

Now that the service is running and in the foreground, I can show you what an empty `ContentObserver` looks like:

```
ContentObserver mContentObserver = new ContentObserver(null) {
    public void onChange(boolean self){
    }
};
```

Each time *any* photo on the phone changes, `onChange` will be called. It is your task, at that time, to determine what change actually took place. You should do this by querying the `ContentProvider` for images that were created after the `lastUpdateTime`. Here's what that looks like in my sample code:

```
Cursor cursor = null;
try {
   cursor = getContentResolver().query(
      MediaStore.Images.Media.EXTERNAL_CONTENT_URI, null,
      MediaStore.Images.Media.DATE_TAKEN + " > "+lastUpdateTime,
      null, null);
} finally {
   if(cursor!= null){
      cursor.close();
   }
}
```

If this looks similar to an SQL database query, it's meant to. I'm specifying the URI that I want information about (all images). The next parameter (to which I pass null) would be my chance to list the specific columns I want to receive. By passing null, I've asked for all of them. Next is the WHERE clause of the query, where I'm asking for every photo created after the lastUpdateTime. Since I don't have any more statements, I'll leave the next parameter null. Finally, the default sorting of results will suffice, so I can pass null for the last parameter as well. Theoretically, the cursor should contain exactly one image. Here's how I process the cursor coming back from the ContentProvider:

```
lastUpdateTime = System.currentTimeMillis();
if(cursor.moveToFirst()){
   Intent i = new Intent(ACTION_PHOTO_TAKEN);
   String imagePath = cursor.getString(
      cursor.getColumnIndex(
         MediaStore.Images.Media.DATA));
   i.putExtra("path", imagePath);
   sendBroadcast(i);
}
```

TIP: Uploading photos: Normally, instead of calling sendBroadcast, I'd spin up another service (or an AsyncTask) to upload the photo to my favorite photo-sharing service. These services tend to change so often that it's probably not worth spelling out exactly how to accomplish such a thing for Twitter, Facebook, Google+, Tumblr, Imgur, and so on. If you want to implement your own, use the photo-downloading IntentService from Chapter 4 as a framework and go from there.

Now that I have the cursor, I can set the new lastUpdateTime. This will ensure that this current picture will not show up in subsequent observer-fired queries. Instead of starting an upload, I'm just sending an alert that a photo was taken and where you can find that new file. if(cursor.moveToFirst()) is a great way to move your cursor to the first item and check if the cursor isn't empty at the same time. If that condition passes, I retrieve the path from the cursor and add it as an extra to my new intent. Last, I'll broadcast the existence of the photo for anyone who might be listening for it.

It's important to call `cursor.close` on every `cursor` you get back from a `ContentProvider`. Otherwise, the system will throw errors at you for leaking memory.

BINDER SERVICE COMMUNICATION

On the very opposite side of the spectrum from intent-based communication is a service controlled through a binder interface. This allows cross-process communication with any other component that binds itself to your service. More than one process or component can bind with any service singleton, but they will, of course, all be accessing the same one.

Binding—and subsequently calling methods directly on the service—requires a few steps to handle the exchange cleanly and efficiently.

1. Create the interface with an AIDL file.
2. Create a service stub to return as the `IBinder` object.
3. Implement a `ServiceConnection` to make the connection with the service.

As you can see, this is not to be embarked upon unless you really need tight integration between your component and the service to which you'd like to bind.

In a later chapter, I'll show you the ins and outs of media playback and recording. To do this correctly, you're going to need the kind of integration that only a service with a bound interface can provide. So, by way of example, I'm going to build a background service with an `IBinder` suitable to play music in the background. For brevity, I'll avoid discussing every single method, but I'll cover a few basic functions and show you how to establish the connection.

CREATING AN AIDL

The AIDL (Android Interface Definition Language) file is your chance to define the interface through which your service can talk to the outside world. In Eclipse, you will place your AIDL files in the same place as the rest of your Java files. In the example project, the `IMusicService.aidl` file is located in the `src/com/peachpit/serviceExample/` directory. In Android Studio, you'll create a new folder at `src/main/aidl/` and place your `IMusicService.aidl` file in there. Once you've created your AIDL file, open it and add the following code to declare an interface:

```
package com.peachpit.serviceExample;
interface IMusicService
{
    void pause();
    void play();
    void setDataSource(in long id);
    String getSongTitle();
}
```

More methods will eventually be needed for a fully functional music service, but for now this will do. When you next compile your project, Android will create an IMusicService.java file (you can find it in Eclipse under the gen package) containing all the Java code required to marshal the appropriate data across processes.

You might be wondering what that in prefix is doing in front of the parameter declaration of setDataSource. This is how you tell the service that, in this case, the service is the roach motel of method calls. The parameter goes in, but it doesn't come out (you won't be modifying or changing it within your service). This allows Android to marshal the variable across the processes once, but it means that it doesn't have to marshal it back out again, saving time and resources.

> **TIP:** Marshaling is the process of turning an object into a form that is suitable for transferring between threads or processes. When a marshaled object is received, it is unmarshaled in order to get a copy of the original object back. In this respect, it is similar to serialization / deserialization.

CREATING ANOTHER SERVICE

You're so good at creating services that I don't even need to walk you through doing it. I'm going to make myself a new service just as I did before. You do the same. But this time, when you declare it, put it in a different process:

```
<service android:name="MusicService"
    android:process=":music_service"/>
```

The colon (:) in the process tells the system to prefix your current package name to it; otherwise, you can name the process anything you want. This way, the system can keep your music service running in the background while, at the same time, being able to shut down your larger application process, which is very handy on resource-constrained phones.

In the new service, I've declared all the same methods I had in the AIDL interface file. It currently looks like this:

```
public class MusicService extends Service{
    private void pause(){
    }
    private void play(){
    }
    public void setDataSource(long id){
    }
    public String getSongTitle(){
        return null;
    }
    @Override
    public IBinder onBind(Intent intent) {
```

```
        return null;
    }
}
```

CREATING THE BINDER AND AIDL STUB

Now that you have an interface and the methods in the service, it's time to connect the two. You'll need to do this using a stub. The stub keeps a weak reference to the service while also implementing your AIDL interface. It's also the object you'll pass back—instead of null—to the onBind call. You can declare it inside your service (although you don't actually have to). Here's what my stub looks like (complete with my new onBind call to return it back to the system):

```
private final IBinder mBinder = new MusicServiceStub(this);
@Override
public IBinder onBind(Intent intent) {
    return mBinder;
}
static class MusicServiceStub extends IMusicService.Stub {
    WeakReference<MusicService> mService;
    MusicServiceStub(MusicService service) {
        mService = new WeakReference<MusicService>(service);
    }
    public void pause(){
        mService.get().pause();
    }
    public void play(){
        mService.get().play();
    }
    public void setDataSource(long id){
        mService.get().setDataSource(id);
    }
    public String getSongTitle(){
        return mService.get().getSongTitle();
    }
}
```

You can see how it extends the IMusicService.Stub class and takes, in its constructor, a reference to the outer service that it wraps in a weak reference. You need to do this because the system may keep a reference to the binder stub long after the service's onDestroy method has been called, and you'll want the garbage collector to be able clean up your service. For the curious, the weak reference allows the wrapped class to be deallocated by the garbage collector if the weak reference is the only remaining reference to it. Quite handy in this case, because it should help us prevent some memory leaks in the future.

You can also see how I'm returning this as the IBinder object when onBind is called. This MusicServiceStub will be the object that other components use to communicate with the service.

BINDING AND COMMUNICATING WITH THE SERVICE

You now have all the components you need to communicate, across a process, with your service. It's time to establish the connection.

I've added two more buttons to my service example activity to bind and unbind from my new skeleton music service. Here's what I've added to my OnClickListener to support them:

```
Intent bindServiceIntent =
    new Intent(getApplicationContext(), MusicService.class);
if(v.getId() == R.id.start_binder_service) {
    bindService(bindServiceIntent, this, Service.BIND_AUTO_CREATE);
} else if(v.getId() == R.id.stop_binder_service) {
    unbindService(this);
}
```

You can see, in the highlighted code, that I'm binding with the service by giving it the following:

- An intent specifying which service I'd like to connect to.
- A reference to a ServiceConnection object (which I'll make my activity implement).
- A flag telling the system how I'd like the service started (in this case, BIND_AUTO_CREATE—meaning that it will create this service if it doesn't exist when you try to bind to it).

Now, my example code won't compile until I actually add an implements ServiceConnection to my activity's class declaration and the required methods that it entails. Here, in all their glory, are my activity's new required methods:

```
IMusicService mService;
@Override
public void onServiceConnected(ComponentName name, IBinder service) {
    mService = IMusicService.Stub.asInterface(service);
    try {
        mService.setDataSource(0);
    } catch (RemoteException re) {
        Log.e("MusicService", "",re);
    }
}
@Override
public void onServiceDisconnected(ComponentName name) {
}
```

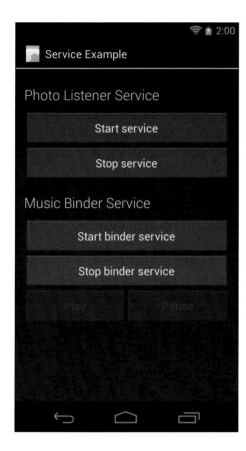

This code might look a little strange, but the `asInterface` call is converting from the `IBinder` object to the `IMusicService` (which I can then make direct calls on). However, each call to the remote service requires that you catch potential `RemoteExceptions` that come up.

That's really all there is to it. Once you've received the `onServiceConnected` call and completed the conversion, you can stash that `MusicService` object for whenever you need it. Just don't forget to unbind it when your `onDestroy` method gets called. I've added Play and Pause buttons to the example code (**Figure 6.2**) so that you can get an idea of how you might interact with the service while it's running. It can be a little tricky to maintain all of the states, but it is an essential tool to have in your Android developer toolbox.

Creating an AIDL and binding to a service in this way is actually one of the more complicated ways to communicate with a service. If you're not going to be building a long-running service in a separate process, this might not be the perfect setup for you. Consider checking the SDK documentation for the locally bound service or messenger patterns.

WRAPPING UP

In this chapter, you learned how to use a simple foreground service to notify you when a photograph is added to Android's ContentProvider. You learned how to start it, place it in the foreground with a notification, and then kill it off when the user no longer wanted it to run. Next, I went from the simple to the complex and showed you how to communicate directly with a service across process boundaries. You did this by creating an AIDL interface, implementing a stub, and then using a ServiceConnection and a bindService call to establish a connection with the service.

The first example was a simple service that does only one thing, while the second example you stormed through was one of the more complex mechanisms that Android can provide. If your arms are long enough (and you're not a *Tyrannosaurus rex*), give yourself a resounding pat on the back.

CHAPTER 7

Many Devices, One Application

Android devices have hundreds of different hardware configurations, from advanced TVs to very basic phones. Writing an application that runs perfectly across the whole spectrum can seem like a daunting task. Android, fortunately, provides many tools to handle the ecosystem on which it runs. In this chapter, I'll show you how to leverage Android's layout folder hierarchy system, configure your manifest to ensure that your application is available only to phones that can run it correctly, and handle older versions of the Android SDK. Android's diversity can be a challenge, but I'll show you how to use the available tools to make it a manageable one. This chapter also covers the secrets of the res/ folder; weeding out devices with the manifest; and accommodating older phones with reflection.

UNCOVERING THE SECRETS OF THE RES/ FOLDER

Earlier, I gave you a basic mapping of what goes where in the res/ folder. In this section, I'll show you its more advanced functions. As always, you can either code this yourself or follow along from the sample code posted at Peachpit.com/androiddevelopanddesign.

LAYOUT FOLDERS

Layout resource folders will be the first technique at your disposal, and it also happens to be one of the most effective. Android will pick layout files from a folder that matches the hardware configuration closest to the one it's running on. Using this technique, you can define multiple screen layouts for any number of different hardware configurations. Let's start with something simple: landscape mode.

Let's say you have a simple screen with two buttons. Here's the XML that produced the two buttons.

```xml
<!--Text view for question and relative layout params omitted-->
<RelativeLayout
    android:id="@+id/button_holder"
    android:layout_centerInParent="true"
    android:layout_width="match_parent"
    android:layout_height="wrap_content"
    android:padding="20dp">

    <Button
        android:id="@+id/yes_button"
        android:layout_width="match_parent"
        android:layout_height="wrap_content"
        android:gravity="center"
        android:padding="15dp"
        android:text="@string/yes_button_text" />

    <Button
        android:id="@+id/no_button"
        android:layout_width="match_parent"
        android:layout_height="wrap_content"
        android:layout_below="@id/yes_button"
        android:gravity="center"
        android:padding="15dp"
        android:text="@string/no_button_text" />
</RelativeLayout>
```

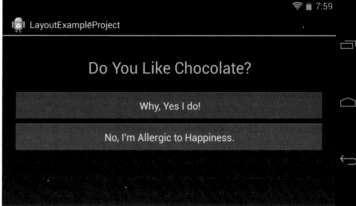

FIGURE 7.1 A simple screen with two buttons   **FIGURE 7.2** The buttons are far too large in landscape mode.

What you see in this code listing shouldn't be anything new, given your experience with the RelativeLayout in previous chapters. I've declared two buttons, pinning the Yes button to the top and aligning the No button below it. When shown in portrait mode, these buttons look simple but pretty good (**Figure 7.1**). While this will win me a design award only if the judges are partially blind, it's a fairly good-looking, simple, and functional screen. But take a look at what happens when I switch it to landscape mode (**Figure 7.2**).

This is, for lack of a better term, ugly. The buttons are far too wide in proportion to both their text and the "Do You Like Chocolate?" question above them. This is exactly the sort of problem that Android's layout folders make easy to solve.

To the fix this graphical mess, I want the buttons to be side by side in landscape mode while still being stacked in portrait mode. There are two approaches to fixing this problem: a slightly heavy-handed method involving setting up a second screen layout for landscape, or using a scalpel to excise and fix only the parts that are broken. Both solutions have their place. And both solutions require a new folder.

THE LANDSCAPE FOLDER

Android allows you to specify different layout folders for various hardware screen configurations. Since both solutions require a `layout-land` folder, let's create it now. Inside your resources folder (`res/`), create a new folder named `layout-land`. Since resource folders are ordered alphabetically, this folder should show directly below the `layout` folder.

USING DIFFERENT FOLDERS

The first example solves the problem by adding an entirely separate layout file to your `layout-land` folder that will take the place of the default layout located in the `layout` folder.

Now we come to the magic part.

Create a new layout file inside the `layout-land` resource folder, and name it the same as the layout file you wish to replace in the `layout` folder. For example, in our project, both of these files are named `activity_main.xml`. With this extra layout file in the `layout-land` folder, Android will use the appropriate layout *automatically* when the device is in landscape mode, no code required!

USING <INCLUDE> FOR SMALL CHANGES

The `<include>` tag is a fantastic way to pull out small portions of your screen that you'd like to tweak and lay out separately. This is the scalpel method. You cut out only the portions you want to render differently, you split them into folder-separated layouts, and you're finished. Which, in this case, is a perfect way to excise the buttons and have them render differently depending on the screen orientation. Here's how to do exactly that.

1. Create a new `button_layout.xml` file in `res/layout-land/`.

   This is the file into which we'll put the landscape-specific layout.

2. Add a `LinearLayout` and two `Buttons` in the new `button_layout.xml` file, and place them next to each other in the new horizontal linear layout. Here's the final contents of my `/layout-land/button_layout.xml`.

   ```xml
   <?xml version="1.0" encoding="utf-8"?>
   <LinearLayout xmlns:android="http://schemas.android.com/apk/res/android"
       android:id="@+id/button_holder"
       android:layout_width="match_parent"
       android:layout_height="wrap_content"
       android:layout_centerInParent="true"
       android:padding="20dp"
       android:orientation="horizontal">

       <Button
           android:id="@+id/yes_button"
           android:layout_width="match_parent"
           android:layout_height="wrap_content"
           android:layout_weight="1"
   ```

```
        android:layout_marginRight="5dp"
        android:gravity="center"
        android:padding="15dp"
        android:text="@string/yes_button_text" />


    <Button
        android:id="@+id/no_button"
        android:layout_width="match_parent"
        android:layout_height="wrap_content"
        android:layout_weight="1"
        android:layout_marginLeft="5dp"
        android:gravity="center"
        android:padding="15dp"
        android:text="@string/no_button_text" />
</LinearLayout>
```

As you can see, I've created a horizontal layout with two buttons to be used in landscape mode.

Don't forget about the portrait layout. If we're going to include a layout, it's got to exist for both the landscape configuration and the default configuration.

3. Create a new button_layout.xml file in /res/layout/ (or you could add it as /res/layout-port/button_layout.xml). I've just copied the original buttons' code and pasted it into a new RelativeLayout:

```
<?xml version="1.0" encoding="utf-8"?>
<RelativeLayout
    xmlns:android="http://schemas.android.com/apk/res/android"
    android:layout_marginBottom="60dp"
    android:layout_width="fill_parent"
    android:layout_height="100dp"
    android:layout_alignParentBottom="true">
    <Button
        android:padding="15dp"
        android:gravity="center"
        android:id="@+id/yes_button"
        android:layout_marginLeft="30dp"
        android:layout_marginRight="30dp"
        android:layout_width="fill_parent"
        android:layout_height="wrap_content"
```

```
      android:layout_above="@+id/no_button"
      android:text="@string/yes_button_text"/>
   <Button
      android:padding="15dp"
      android:gravity="center"
      android:id="@+id/no_button"
      android:layout_marginLeft="30dp"
      android:layout_marginRight="30dp"
      android:layout_width="fill_parent"
      android:layout_height="wrap_content"
      android:text="@string/no_button_text"
      android:layout_alignParentBottom="true"/>
</RelativeLayout>
```

At this point, you've created two layouts: one for portrait and one for landscape.

4. You can now modify your original XML with an `include` so it looks like this:

```
<?xml version="1.0" encoding="utf-8"?>
<RelativeLayout xmlns:android="http://schemas.android.com/apk/res/android"
   android:layout_width="match_parent"
   android:layout_height="match_parent">

   <TextView
      android:layout_width="match_parent"
      android:layout_height="wrap_content"
      android:layout_above="@+id/button_holder"
      android:gravity="center"
      android:text="@string/question_text"
      android:textSize="15dp" />

   <include layout="@layout/button_layout" />

</RelativeLayout>
```

With the `<include ... />` tag in place (instead of a single button definition), Android will grab the button_layout.xml file that corresponds to the screen configuration. If it can't find one, it will default back to what's in /res/layout.

FIGURE 7.3 No awards for design, but much better.

MERGING

You don't have to wrap your excised views in a new ViewGroup (RelativeLayout in the previous example) for them to be included (as I did here). If you don't want to add another layout to the mix but would like to bring in a series of views from other XML files, simply wrap them in a <merge> tag.

```
<merge xmlns:android="http://schemas.android.com/apk/res/android">
<!-- views go here -->
</merge>
```

This will allow you to include views without adding another layout to your view hierarchy. Be careful, though—the children in the merge layout will inherit parent properties from the layout they are merged into. Merging into a LinearLayout can have very different results (versus a RelativeLayout) if you don't plan this out ahead of time.

Now, with this new code, the landscape mode looks much better (**Figure 7.3**).

Are there things that could be improved? Sure! Now, however, you know how to specify that parts of your user interface should change as the screen's hardware configuration changes.

WHAT CAN YOU DO BEYOND LANDSCAPE?

Lots. You can add suffixes to layout folders to account for just about everything. Here are a few I use on a regular basis:

- `layout-small`, `layout-normal`, `layout-large`, `layout-xlarge`

  The size modifier accounts for the physical size of the screen. Devices that would use the small layout folder are typically very old or very strange pieces of hardware, at least until Android-powered watches become popular. Most modern phones fit the `layout-normal` category, while many tablets are considered `xlarge`. Google keeps a great breakdown of all the various screen configurations at http://developer.android.com/resources/dashboard/screens.html.

- `layout-ldpi`, `layout-mdpi`, `layout-hdpi`, `layout-xhdpi`, `layout-sw600dp`

  The dpi, or dots per inch, of the device is a measurement of screen *density*. Screens with high densities (240 dpi) would pull from the layout folder `layout-hdpi`. Devices whose smallest width (`sw`) is 600dp or greater would pull from the `layout-sw600dp` folder, which is the generally accepted qualifier for 7-inch tablets such as the Nexus 7.

- `layout-large-hdpi-land`

  You can also mix and match the suffixes. This suffix would be used for phones that have large screens and high resolution and that are in landscape mode. Get creative, but remember that just because you *can* get very specific about screen configurations, it doesn't mean you *should*.

THE FULL SCREEN DEFINE

Just as you can place separate layout files to be referenced in `<include>` for different hardware configurations, so can you define a completely different screen in the `layout-land` folder for the system to use in landscape mode. This might seem like the best course of action at first, but it is less than ideal for several reasons.

- It involves a lot of typing.

  Instead of defining two small parts that change based on the screen configuration, you have to make and test more than one entire screen layout.

- Making changes can be painful.

  With many hardware configurations comes a plethora of different screens. Were you to fully lay out a screen for every configuration, you'd have a nightmare on your hands when your designer wants to remove or add a button. You would have to add it separately to each XML file for every single screen configuration.

Those two things aside, sometimes you really do need a completely separate layout for a different hardware or screen configuration. Try to modify small parts when you can, but don't be afraid to crack your knuckles and make a totally new screen layout when it's necessary.

To make a new layout of the "chocolate" example, you can simply make a second `two_buttons.xml` file in `/res/layout-land` and configure the screen in any way you like.

Then the call to setContentView in the onCreate method of your activity will, like include, find the right resource for the right screen configuration.

HOW CAN THIS POSSIBLY WORK?

That's a great question that I'm glad you asked only at the end of the section. Because it separates layout files from activities, Android can have any number of different layouts for the myriad of possible screen configurations. You simply specify the layout name, and Android goes off in search of the correct XML file to show the user. To keep this process running smoothly, keep the following things in mind:

- The layouts *must* share the same name.

    Android can only find the layout XML by name. As long as the layout files have the exact same filename, it will locate the version in your landscape (or any other) folder.

- Make sure that the IDs for your individual views are consistent.

    Remember that your activity calls findViewById in order to manipulate and interact with onscreen objects. The activity shouldn't care where a view is to register a click listener, set an image, or pull data from an EditText.

- Try not to move views around in your activity's Java code.

    Your activity shouldn't try to change the position of things onscreen. While in portrait mode, the button might be at point (330, 120); it will be somewhere totally different in landscape mode. In this situation, adding more screen layouts will require also adding the corresponding movement code to your activity, and this can become time consuming.

BE CAREFUL

Debugging layout issues across many linked layout files can be exhausting (I've done it), so keep your layouts as stretchy and dynamic as you possibly can. If your designs are done well, they should be able to handle many screen resolutions automatically with good use of linear and relative layouts. Fall back on includes and multiple layout folders only when dynamic layouts can't do the job. There will be times, however, when one layout doesn't do all screens justice. When this happens, make your breakouts as small and efficient as possible. Don't hesitate to use this amazing layout tool, but be careful not to use it too much.

LIMITING ACCESS TO YOUR APP TO DEVICES THAT WORK

Your Android application may, in a lot of cases, require some very specific hardware in order to work correctly. I imagine that users who, for example, download a camera app to a device that doesn't have a camera will have a very poor experience.

THE <USES> TAG

Android gives you an avenue to tell the marketplace which devices it should allow to download and purchase your application. This is done with the <uses> tag in your AndroidManifest.xml file.

If, for example, your app requires the device to have a camera, you should add the following line to your manifest:

```
<uses-feature android:name="android.hardware.camera"
    android:required="true"/>
```

This line tells Android that the application should not be installed on a device without a camera, because it's required for correct operation. You can, on the flip side, declare that your app use a particular piece of hardware but degrade appropriately if it's not there. An image-editing app might want the camera, but if the camera's not there it may still function by modifying images saved from the web in the device's built-in gallery. You tell the system this by declaring the hardware as used but setting the requirement to false:

```
<uses-feature android:name="android.hardware.camera"
    android:required="false"/>
```

There are a host of hardware features you can set. It's probably best to check the documentation for the full list (http://developer.android.com/guide/topics/manifest/uses-feature-element.html).

SDK VERSION NUMBER

You can also declare which versions of the SDK your application supports. You do this by declaring <uses-sdk> in your manifest. In fact, if you created your project using your IDE or command-line tools, you already have a basic declaration:

```
<uses-sdk android:minSdkVersion="10" />
```

You can add minimum and maximum supported SDKs if there are classes or objects you rely on that aren't available on older devices. You can, however, block out older and newer versions of the SDK with a declaration that looks like this:

```
<uses-sdk
    android:maxSdkVersion="14"
    android:minSdkVersion="9" />
```

This will tell Google Play to list the associated application for devices that are SDK 9: Android 2.3 (code name Gingerbread) and above. It will also block devices greater than SDK 14: Android 4.0 (code name Ice Cream Sandwich) from running your software. Further, if you try to load the app through a web link, the downloader will block the install on the grounds that the application isn't supported.

It's worth mentioning that this sort of heavy-handed blocking should really be a last-ditch effort. If you can make your application work well with both the latest and oldest devices, you should. With this declaration, you can limit who is allowed to install your app.

HANDLING CODE IN OLDER ANDROID VERSIONS

I can't tell you how many times I've found the *perfect* Android SDK class to solve some annoying problem, only to find out that its use is limited to the latest version of the SDK. There is one trick you can use when faced with code that will compile only on later versions of Android: reflection.

While reflection is in no way unique to Android (it's built into Java), it is something you can use to protect older phones from newfangled classes and methods.

SHAREDPREFERENCES AND APPLY

Long ago, in a galaxy that's actually quite close, Google figured out that writing to disk on the main thread is a bad thing for performance. During this discovery, they found that the SharedPreferences (something that's typically used to save user settings and preferences) do actually write to disk when you save them through their commit method. You'll see what I'm talking about in the following method, which saves a username to the preferences:

```
public void setUsername(String username){
    SharedPreferences prefs =
        PreferenceManager.getDefaultSharedPreferences(this);
    Editor ed = prefs.edit();
    ed.putString("username", username);
    ed.commit();
}
```

This works just fine, but as it turns out, commit writes to the disk, and calling this on the main thread is a no-no (for reasons we've discussed at length). In SDK version 9, however, Google introduced the apply method to the SharedPreferences Editor class. Again, this is great, but there's a catch: Any device that tries to use a class containing the apply method will throw a validation exception and crash. So how, you might be wondering, do you use apply on Android SDK 9 (2.3.3) and higher without breaking any 2.2 (or earlier) devices?

Sometimes, you'll need to gate off certain functionality for certain versions of Android. As in the example, a function may not exist, but there may be certain bugs that are only present on certain platforms. Using the following two variables will give you the control you need to apply specific behavior to specific platforms.

- `Build.VERSION.SDK_INT` is an integer representing the value of the SDK that the devices is currently running.

- `Build.VERSION_CODE.GINGERBREAD` is an integer constant provided to you by the system. All versions of Android are represented in the `VERSION_CODE` constants, up to the SDK target that you are compiling with. You could replace this constant with the number 9, but it would not be as readable in your code base.

VERSION CHECK YOUR TROUBLES AWAY

The solution for this problem, and indeed all problems with later declared SDK methods, is to access them conditionally by checking the API version at runtime. Runtime checking is a great way to handle these kinds of situations.

Ideally, I'd like to call apply if it's available (SDK 9 and higher) but fall back to commit if apply is going to cause problems. Here's the new version of setUsername to do exactly that:

```
public void setUserName(String username){
    SharedPreferences prefs =
        PreferenceManager.getDefaultSharedPreferences(this);
    Editor ed = prefs.edit();
    ed.putString("username", username);

    if(Build.VERSION.SDK_INT >= Build.VERSION_CODES.GINGERBREAD){
        ed.apply();
    }else{
        ed.commit();
    }
}
```

While this method starts the same as the previous one—getting the Editor and using it to save the string—it diverges when it comes time to save that username.

`Build.VERSION.SDK_INT` will always refer to the current build number of the device that the application is running on. If the device is running 2.3, it will return 9; if the device is running 4.2.2, it will return 17; and so on. This number will correspond with the constants in `Build.VERSION_CODES`, which is a convenient way to check the compatibility of the OS with the code you are trying to run.

In this code, we are checking whether the OS version is at least Gingerbread. If it is, we are going to use the `apply` method; otherwise, we are going to use the `commit` method. This technique has a variety of use cases, such as only using the new `ActionBar` APIs that were added in API 11 and API 14.

ALWAYS KEEP AN EYE ON API LEVELS

In the Android documentation, each class and method has a small gray label reading "Since: API Level #" on the right-hand side. If that number is higher than the system you'd like to support, you may need to re-evaluate using that class or method.

Reflection allows you to have the best of both worlds. You can use these latest methods on newer devices that support them, while gracefully degrading on devices that don't.

Keep in mind, however, that reflection is slow and potentially error prone, so use it sparingly and with care. If you're going to be frequently using a class or method that has two different implementations (`Contacts`, for example), consider using a Factory pattern to load different classes instead. That is, write two `Adapter` classes for each version of the class (one for the old, one for the new), and use your Factory to return whichever one is supported. You can always find out which SDK your device is running by checking `android.os.Build.Version.SDK`.

WRAPPING UP

In this chapter, you learned how to handle diversity in screen resolution, density, and configuration. You did this through advanced use of the layout folders, the `<include>` tag, and Android's XML layout system. Then you learned how to tell Android which device features you require by putting declarations in the manifest. Last, you learned about using OS version checking to take advantage of advanced methods when they're available and to avoid them when they're not.

Given all these tools, you should be ready to bring your killer mobile application into play on the tremendous number of devices—from refrigerators to phones to televisions—available to you on the Android platform.

In any case, monotony is boring. Different devices allow for innovation, greater user choice, and funny-looking screen protectors. Now that you're equipped to handle it, you'll be scaling resources and rocking the landscape mode with ease.

CHAPTER 8

Movies and Music

Support for media, both audio and visual, will hopefully be an essential part of your next immersive Android application. Both industries are on the forefront of mobile usage, and many modern mobile applications are leveraging this technology to build thoughtful and engaging applications. To this end, I'll get you started with the basics for Android's video and music libraries in this chapter. I'll also point out a few things you'll need to be aware of as you build a background media playback service: movies, music playback, background service, and what to watch out for.

MOVIES

Movie playback on an Android device boils down to the `VideoView` class. In this section, I'll use a simple example application that will play through every video saved on a phone's SD card. Here is the general process:

- I'll use the `ContentProvider` (something you'll remember from our brief discussion in Chapter 6 when we uploaded the most recent photo) to request every video saved to the user's external card.

- After loading a `Cursor` (Android's query result data object) with all the device's videos, I'll need a method to play the next one.

- I'll set up an activity as a listener so that when video playback is complete, I can call my `playNextVideo` method and move on to the next video in the cursor.

- Last, I'll clean up after my cursor when the user leaves the playback screen.

Before I can do any of these things, however, I need to place a `VideoView` on my main layout to work with.

ADDING A VIDEOVIEW

Placing a `VideoView` onscreen is as simple as adding it to your XML layout. Here's what my `main.xml` file now looks like:

```xml
<?xml version="1.0" encoding="utf-8"?>
<LinearLayout xmlns:android="http://schemas.android.com/apk/res/android"
    android:orientation="vertical"
    android:layout_width="match_parent"
    android:layout_height="match_parent">

    <VideoView
        android:id="@+id/my_video_view"
        android:layout_gravity="center"
        android:layout_width="match_parent"
        android:layout_height="match_parent" />

</LinearLayout>
```

Once the video view is in the screen's layout, you can retrieve it, as you would any other view, with `findViewById`. I'm going to need access to the video view later when it's time to switch videos. Instead of retrieving the view with `findViewById` each time, I'll add a private data member to my `Activity` class. Next, I'll need to configure the video player.

SETTING UP FOR THE VIDEOVIEW

In the following code listing, I'm doing many normal onCreate sorts of things.

```
VideoView mVideoView;
@Override
public void onCreate(Bundle savedInstanceState) {
    super.onCreate(savedInstanceState);
    setContentView(R.layout.activity_main);

    mVideoView = (VideoView) findViewById(R.id.my_video_view);
    mVideoView.setOnCompletionListener(this);


}
```

Here I'm setting the content view, retrieving and caching the video view with findViewById, and setting my activity as the video view's onCompletionListener.

In order for the activity to pass itself into the VideoView as the onCompletionListener, I have to extend OnCompletionListener and implement my own onCompletion method. Here is what I've added to my activity:

```
public class MainActivity extends Activity
        implements OnCompletionListener{
    @Override
    public void onCompletion(MediaPlayer mp) {
    }
    //Rest of Activity code omitted
}
```

I now have a configured, yet very simplistic, video player. You'll most likely want to have visual onscreen controls. Android's VideoView allows you to implement and set up a MediaController for the VideoView class. If you're looking to go further into video playback after this chapter, this would be an excellent place to start.

GETTING MEDIA TO PLAY

Now that my video view is ready to roll, I can start hunting for things for it to actually play. For this simple example, I'm going to play every video on the device one after another until they're all finished. To achieve this, I'll use Android's media ContentProvider (accessed with a call to getContentResolver). I'll show you the code and then dig into some specifics. Here's what onCreate looks like with the new code to fetch a cursor with all the media objects:

```java
@Override
public void onCreate(Bundle savedInstanceState) {
   super.onCreate(savedInstanceState);
   setContentView(R.layout.activity_main);

   mVideoView = (VideoView) findViewById(R.id.my_video_view);
   mVideoView.setOnCompletionListener(this);

   requestVideosFromPhone();
}

private void requestVideosFromPhone() {

   new AsyncTask<Void, Void, Cursor>() {
      @Override
      protected Cursor doInBackground(Void... params) {

         String projection[] = new String[] { Video.Media.DATA };
         final Cursor c = getContentResolver().query(
              Video.Media.EXTERNAL_CONTENT_URI,
              projection,
              null, null, null);
         return c;
      }

      @Override
      protected void onPostExecute(Cursor result) {
         if (result != null) {
            mMediaCursor = result;
            mMediaCursor.moveToFirst();
            playNextVideo();
         }
      }
   }.execute();
}
```

As you can see, I'm still fetching and caching the video view, but now I'm firing off an AsyncTask that will query Android's ContentProvider for the Video.Media.DATA column of all media rows that are videos. Don't let it scare you that I created an anonymous inner AsyncTask by calling new AsyncTask from inside the function. This technique is a great way to kick things off the main thread without having to declare an entire subclass class for it. That query inside the AsyncTask is fairly simple in that I want all videos on the external drive (SD card), and I only care about the data column for all those rows. This column for any particular row should always contain the path to the actual media content on disk. It's this path that I'll eventually hand off to the VideoView for playback.

Note that it is possible to pass URIs to the video view. The video playback mechanism will find the path to the object for you. I would, however, like to show you the harder way so that you'll be more informed.

The Cursor object (a class Android uses to wrap database query responses) can be null if the external media card is removed (or mounted into USB storage mode), so I'll need to check for a null cursor or one with no results before moving on. Typically in this case, I'd display a message to the user about their SD card being unavailable, but I'll leave that task up to your imagination.

Last, I'll get and cache the column index for the data row. This will make it easier for my playNextVideo method to interact with the cursor's results.

ADDING PERMISSIONS

Starting in Android 4.4, the permission READ_EXTERNAL_STORAGE, which has been in since API 16, is being enforced. To future proof your application and let your users know what permissions you are using, add this permission into your manifest:

```
<manifest>
  ...
  <uses-permission
    android:name="android.permission.READ_EXTERNAL_STORAGE"/>
  ...
</manifest>
```

LOADING AND PLAYING MEDIA

At this point, you have a video view, a cursor full of media to play, and a listener configured to tell you when media playback is finished. Let's put the final piece into the game, the code in playNextVideo:

```
private void playNextVideo() {
    if (!mMediaCursor.isAfterLast()) {
        final String path = mMediaCursor.getString(
            mMediaCursor.getColumnIndexOrThrow(
                Video.Media.DATA));

        Toast.makeText(getBaseContext(),
            "Playing: " + path, Toast.LENGTH_SHORT).show();
        mVideoView.setVideoPath(path);
        mVideoView.start();

        // Advance the cursor
        mMediaCursor.moveToNext();
    } else {
        Toast.makeText(getBaseContext(),
            "End of Line.", Toast.LENGTH_SHORT).show();
    }
}
```

My first task is to check if the cursor is after the last piece of media and make sure we haven't run out of stuff to play. When I know I've got a valid row from the cursor, I can tell the video view what it should render next. Video views can accept both a path defined as a string as well as the URI for a piece of media declared in the content provider. As I mentioned earlier, the data column of the cursor contains the file path to the media itself. I'll pull this out of the Cursor, hand it off to the video view, and then start playback. After playback has started, I will advance the cursor to the next position so that it is ready for checking when the current video finishes.

TIP: You're not limited to just file paths—you can hand the video view a URL, and it will query and play the media found there.

Recall that earlier I registered my activity as the OnCompletionListener for the video view so that when a video is finished it will notify me via the OnCompletion call. In that method, I just need to call back into my playNextVideo code and we're playing!

```
@Override
public void onCompletion(MediaPlayer mp) {
    playNextVideo();
}
```

At this point, the pieces are in place, videos play, and you're almost done!

CLEANUP

You've seen me do this at least once before, but it's always important to close any cursors you request from the content provider. In past cases, I've requested data with a query, pulled out the relevant information, and immediately closed the cursor. In this case, however, I need to keep the cursor around for when the video change has to occur. This does not get me off the hook; I still need to close it down, so I'll need to add that code to my activity's onDestroy method:

```
@Override
public void onDestroy() {
    if (mMediaCursor != null) {
        mMediaCursor.close();
    }
}
```

THE REST, AS THEY SAY, IS UP TO YOU

I've shown you the very basics of loading and playing video content. Now it's time for you to explore it on your own. Think about loading a video from a remote location (hint: encoding a URL as a URI) or building a progress bar (hint: getCurrentProgress calls on the VideoView).

Because errors are to media playback as swearing is to sailors, registering for an onErrorListener is never a bad idea. Android will, if you pass it a class that implements the OnErrorListener interface, tell you if it has hiccups playing your media files. As always, check the documentation for more information on playback.

MUSIC

Music playback, in general, revolves around the `MediaPlayer` class. This is in a sense very similar to what you've just done with the video view (except you don't need a `View` object to render into).

Media players, if used to play music, should end up in their own services, with one notable exception: games and application sound effects. Building a sound effect example will make for a very simple way to get into the basics of audio playback.

MEDIAPLAYER AND STATE

You do not simply walk into Mordor. Similarly, you do not simply run about playing things willy-nilly. It requires care, attention to detail, and an understanding of the media player's states. Here they are, in the order you're most likely to encounter them:

- **Idle.** In this state, the `MediaPlayer` doesn't know anything and, consequently, cannot actually do anything. To move on to the initialized state, you'll need to tell it which file it's going to play. This is done through the `setDataSource` method.

- **Initialized.** At this point, the media player knows what you'd like it to play, but it hasn't acquired the data to do so. This is particularly important to understand when dealing with playing remote audio from a URL. Calling `prepare` or `prepareAsync` will move it into the prepared state. It will also load enough data from either the file system or the Internet to be ready for playback.

- **Prepared.** After calling `prepare` or `prepareAsync` (and getting a callback), your media player is ready to rock! At this point, you can call `seek` (to move the playhead) or `start` (to begin playback).

- **Playing.** Audio is pumping, people are dancing (OK, maybe not), and life is good. In this state, you can call `pause` to halt the audio or `seek` to move the play position. You end the party by calling `stop`, which will move the media player back to the initialized state.

Just because you've run out of media to play doesn't mean your player drops into the idle state. It will keep the current file loaded if you want to call `start` (which will restart the audio from the beginning) or `seek` (to move the playhead to a particular place). Only when you call `stop` or `reset` does the `MediaPlayer` clear its buffers and return to the initialized state, ready for you to call `prepare` again.

PLAYING A SOUND

At its most straightforward, media playback is actually quite easy. Android gives you helper methods to shepherd your media player from the idle state to the prepared state if you can specify a file or resource `id` right away. In this example case, you can record your own WAV file or use the beeeep file that I included in the example project. When you have the sound file, add the file to a new resource folder called `raw/`, which you should create at `/res/raw/`. Any asset that you want to be placed in your application, such as text files, sound files, or anything else that doesn't make sense for the normal resource hierarchy, should exist here so the application can reference it and load it directly.

Further, I've added a button (which you should be a pro at by now) that, when pressed, will play the recorded audio. Once the button is defined (`R.id.beep_button`) in the `main.xml` layout file and the audio `beeeep.wav` file is placed in the `raw/` folder, the following code should work like a charm:

```
MediaPlayer mBeeper;
@Override
    public void onCreate(Bundle savedInstanceState) {
        super.onCreate(savedInstanceState);
        setContentView(R.layout.activity_main);
        Button beep = (Button) findViewById(R.id.beep_button);
        beep.setOnClickListener(this);
        mBeeper = MediaPlayer.create(this, R.raw.beeeep);  }
```

As you can see, I'm retrieving the beep_button from the `activity_main.xml` layout (which I told the activity would be my screen's layout) and setting my activity as the click listener for the button. Last, I use the media player's `create` helper method to initialize and prepare the media player with the `beeeep.wav` file from the `raw/` directory.

PLAYING A SOUND EFFECT

Remember that loading media, even from the `res/` folder, can take some time. With this in mind, I've added the media player as a private data member to my `Activity` class. This means I can load it once in my `onCreate` method and then use it every time the user presses the button. Speaking of button pressing, here's the code to play the sound effect when the button is pressed:

```
@Override
public void onClick(View v) {
    mBeeper.start();
}
```

CLEANUP

In order to be a good citizen, there's one more step you need to take: releasing your resources! That's right, when your activity closes down, you need to tell the media player that you're finished with it, like so:

```
@Override
public void onDestroy(){
  if(mBeeper != null){
    mBeeper.stop();
    mBeeper.release();
    mBeeper = null;
  }
}
```

Checking for null before performing the cleanup is a good precaution. If, for whatever reason, there isn't enough memory to load the resource or it fails for another reason, you won't have any null pointer exceptions on your hands.

IT REALLY IS THAT SIMPLE

There's nothing complex about simple sound effect playback. Once you have a media player in the prepared state, you can call start on it as many times as you like to produce the desired effect. Just remember to clean it up once you're finished. Your users will thank you later. Now let's move on to something a little more tricky.

LONGER-RUNNING MUSIC PLAYBACK

You didn't think I'd let you off that easy, did you? Remember two chapters ago when I showed you how to build a service in a separate process by using an AIDL file? I told you you'd need it for longer-running music playback. Here's a quick recap of that process:

1. Create a service, define a few methods to control music playback, and declare the service in your manifest.

2. Create an Android Interface Definition Language (AIDL) file to define how the service will talk to any of the activities.

3. Bind an activity to the service, and, when the callback is hit, save the binder in order to call the service's methods.

   If most, or any, of those steps don't make sense, take a gander back at Chapter 6.

   In this section, I'll show you how to turn the empty service into one that actually plays music in the background. The example music service will have methods to pause, play, set a data source, and ask it what the title of the current song is. To show you this service in practice, I'll have my activity play the most recently added song on my new background music service.

BINDING TO THE MUSIC SERVICE

There is a little overlap here with Chapter 6, but it's worth covering how this works again before I dive into the music service itself. I've added the following code to the onCreate method of our handy MusicExampleActivity.

```
public void onCreate(Bundle savedInstanceState) {
    //Button code omitted
    Intent serviceIntent = new Intent(
        getApplicationContext(), MusicService.class);
    startService(serviceIntent);
    bindService(serviceIntent, this, Service.START_STICKY);
}
```

You'll notice that I'm actually starting the service before I attempt to bind to it. Although you can ask the bind service call to start the service for you, this is not a good idea when building a music service. That's because when you unbind from the service, which you must do whenever your activity is destroyed, it will shut the service down. This, as you might imagine, would be bad if you'd like music to continue playing in the background after your activity has closed.

FINDING THE MOST RECENT TRACK

In the activity's onResume() method I've added a call to a function named requestMost RecentAudio, which will query Android's content provider for the most recent track. Since this is in onResume, this will be called every time the app returns from the background.

I've also added a button to my screen that, when the query returns with some media, will become enabled via a BroadcastReceiver catching an intent from the MusicService, allowing you to click and play it (we will cover that in a few pages). Assuming it has both a track to play and a valid service, I can start playing music. Here's the code that runs when the application hits onResume:

```
@Override
protected void onResume() {
    super.onResume();

    // Register IntentFilters to listen for Broadcasts from the
    // MusicService
    IntentFilter filter = new IntentFilter();
    filter.addAction(MusicService.PLAYING);
    filter.addAction(MusicService.PLAYBACK_PREPARED);
    registerReceiver(mPlayPauseReceiver, filter);
```

```
    // Disable the button until media is prepared
    mPlayPauseButton.setEnabled(false);
    mPlayPauseButton.setText("Preparing...");

    requestMostRecentAudio();
}
/**
 * Request the most recently added audio file from the system
 */
private void requestMostRecentAudio() {

    // The columns which to return
    String[] projection = new String[] {
        MediaStore.Audio.Media._ID,
        MediaStore.Audio.Media.DATE_ADDED };

    // The order in which to return the results
    String sortOrder =
        MediaStore.Audio.Media.DATE_ADDED + " Desc Limit 1";

    CursorLoader cursorLoader = new CursorLoader(this,
            MediaStore.Audio.Media.EXTERNAL_CONTENT_URI,
            projection,
            null,
            null,
            sortOrder);

    cursorLoader.registerListener(R.id.id_music_loader, this);
    cursorLoader.startLoading();
}
```

In this code, I'm using a cursor loader to fetch my rather bizarre query. I'm asking the content provider for all possible audio tracks, but I'm sorting the results in descending order of their addition date (that is, when they were added to the phone) and limiting it to one result. This will, when the loader finishes, return a cursor with one record (the most recent song added to the library).

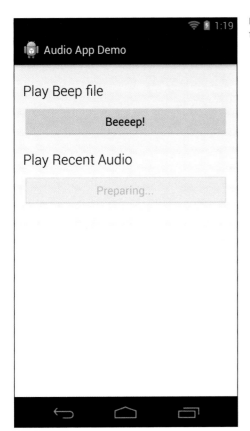

FIGURE 8.1 Keep the button disabled until a success-ful broadcast from the music service is received.

LISTENING FOR INTENTS

To make sure our UI properly reflects when media is ready to be played (**Figure 8.1**), we are going to listen for a broadcast intent from the service. There are a few ways to accomplish this task, but I find that the broadcast intent communication paradigm is an effective way to get messages from one part of your app to another.

```
/**
 * Catch Broadcasts from the MediaService indicating what state the button
should reflect
 */
private BroadcastReceiver mPlayPauseReceiver = new BroadcastReceiver() {
   @Override
   public void onReceive(Context context, Intent intent) {
      final String action = intent.getAction();
      if (MusicService.PLAYING.equals(action)) {
```

```
    try {
       mPlayPauseButton.setText(
           "Pause " + mService.getSongTitle());
    } catch (RemoteException e) {
       e.printStackTrace();
    }

  } else if (MusicService.PLAYBACK_PREPARED.equals(action)) {
     mPlayPauseButton.setText("Play");
     mPlayPauseButton.setEnabled(true);
  }
 }
};
```

The intent communication is pretty straightforward, and in this instance we are using the action of the broadcast intent to determine what behavior we should be applying to the button. If the action is MusicService.PLAYING, indicating that the music is playing, we want to show the pause button with the name of the song that is playing. Otherwise, we want to show the user the play button and make sure it's enabled so they can click it.

When the cursor with my data is ready, my activity's onLoadComplete will be called, at which point I can tell my music service what to play:

```
@Override
public void onLoadComplete(Loader<Cursor> loader, Cursor cursor) {

  if (loader.getId() == R.id.id_music_loader) {
    if (cursor == null || !cursor.moveToFirst()) {
      Toast.makeText(getBaseContext(),
        "No Music to Play",
```

```
          Toast.LENGTH_LONG).show();
      return;
   } else if (mService == null) {
      Toast.makeText(getBaseContext(),
         "No Service to play Music!", Toast.LENGTH_LONG).show();
      return;
   }
   try {
      long id = cursor.getLong(
         cursor.getColumnIndexOrThrow(
            MediaStore.Audio.Media._ID));
      mService.setDataSource(id);
   } catch (RemoteException e) {
      Log.e(TAG, "Failed to set data source", e);
```

```
}
```

allback, I'll first need to check if it actually found any data.
By   ToFirst()), I'm moving to the first and only record in the
c   re there actually is a record for me to look at. (If the cursor is
empty, moveToFirst will return false.)

Next, I'll need to make sure that my service bind in the onCreate method was successful.
Once I know that the service is valid, I'll finally get the media ID by calling getLong on the
cursor to acquire the media's unique ID. It is with this ID that I'll tell the music service via
setDataSource what it should play.

PLAYING THE AUDIO IN THE SERVICE

Now that you can see how the ID is acquired, I'll switch over to the music service and show
you how the handoff occurs over there. Here's what setDataSource looks like from the service's perspective (which we defined the skeleton for earlier):

```
private MediaPlayer mPlayer;
private String mCurrentTitle;
private String mDataSource;

private void setDataSource(long id) {

   // We only want these columns
```

```java
        String[] projection = {
          MediaStore.Audio.Media._ID,
          MediaStore.Audio.Media.DATA,
          MediaStore.Audio.Media.TITLE };

        // The "WHERE" clause, excluding there WHERE
        String selection = MediaStore.Audio.Media._ID + "=?";

        // The arguments for the selection
        String[] selectionArgs = new String[] { String.valueOf(id) };

        final Cursor c = getContentResolver().query(
            MediaStore.Audio.Media.EXTERNAL_CONTENT_URI,
            projection,
            selection,
            selectionArgs,
            null);

        if (c != null && c.moveToFirst()) {
          try {
            mDataSource = c.getString(
              c.getColumnIndexOrThrow(
                MediaStore.Audio.Media.DATA));
            mCurrentTitle = c.getString(
              c.getColumnIndexOrThrow(
                MediaStore.Audio.Media.TITLE));
            prepareMedia();

          } finally {
            c.close();
          }
        }
      }
      /**
       * Prepares Media for playback
       */
      private void prepareMedia() {
        mPlayer.reset();
        try {
```

It's worth noting, again, that I've taken the harder of two routes here. Instead of querying the content provider for the exact media path, I could build a URI for the media in question and hand it off. I've taken what may be a slightly more complex route to playback only so that when you'd like to get to the file itself, you'll know how.

```java
    mPlayer.setDataSource(mDataSource);
} catch (IllegalStateException e) {
    // In a bad state!
    e.printStackTrace();
} catch (IOException e) {
    // Couldn't find the file!
    e.printStackTrace();
}
// Reset the player back to the beginning
mPlayer.prepareAsync();
mPlayer.setOnPreparedListener(
    new MediaPlayer.OnPreparedListener() {
    @Override
    public void onPrepared(MediaPlayer mp) {
        // Send broadcast so the activity can update its
        // button text
        sendBroadcast(new Intent(PLAYBACK_PREPARED));
    }
});
}
```

While this code is a little bit long, most of it should look similar to tasks you've already done.

1. I'm querying the content provider for the id passed into the method.

2. I'm making sure that the music is actually there first by checking if the cursor came back null (which can happen if the SD card has been removed). I'm also checking that there's a valid row in the cursor.

3. When I'm sure the cursor is valid and contains the data for a song to play, I call prepareMedia, which is a method I created to prepare the media player for playback with the new data source. This method will reset the player (in case it was already playing something else), set the data source for it, and tell the media player to prepare. Once these methods are finished, the media player is ready to start playback.

With that, your service is ready to go when the activity calls play.

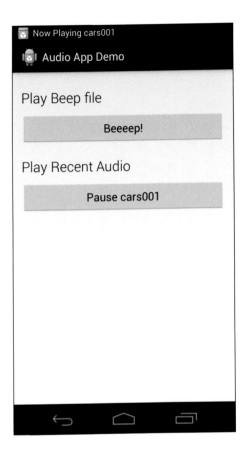

FIGURE 8.2 Recent audio will show in the notification bar while it's playing.

Now Playing cars001

Audio App Demo

Play Beep file

Beeeep!

Play Recent Audio

Pause cars001

PLAY TIME

Now that the service has a data source and is prepared, the activity can call play, which will trigger the following code to run and post a notification to the status bar (**Figure 8.2**):

```
/**
 * Begin or resume playback
 */
private void play() {

  if (mPlayer != null) {
    mPlayer.start();
  }
  // Place a notification in the bar so we can run without being
  // killed by the system
  Notification notification =
  buildSimpleNotification("Now Playing ", getSongTitle());
```

```
startForeground(1, notification);

    // Send broadcast so the activity can update its button text
    sendBroadcast(new Intent(PLAYING));
}
```

You'll need to start media playback and make sure the service switches to running in the foreground. buildSimpleNotification is a method I defined back in Chapter 6 that builds an icon for the status bar to keep your service alive. If you need a refresher on how to put services into foreground mode, review Chapter 6 or look at the sample code for this chapter.

Lastly, I send a broadcast intent letting anyone who is listening know that we have started playing. This is how we will adjust the state of our play button back in our main activity.

ALL GOOD THINGS MUST END END... HOPEFULLY

At some point, the music has to stop—either because it's run out of songs to play or because the user has killed it off. Because I want the service to last beyond the run of my activity, I'll need to have the service close itself down after it has finished playing its media. You can find the appropriate time to shut down the service by registering it as an onCompletionListener with the media player. The line of code looks like this:

```
mPlayer.setOnCompletionListener(this);
```

You can call it at any point after the player is created. Of course, your service will need to implement OnCompletionListener and have the correct onCompletion method.

```
@Override
public void onCompletion(MediaPlayer mp) {
    performStop();
}
/**
 * Stop and reset the playback
 */
private void performStop() {

    if (mPlayer.isPlaying()) {
        mPlayer.stop();
    }

    // Prepare media for the next playback
    prepareMedia();

    // Remove our notification since we aren't playing
```

```
    stopForeground(true);
    stopSelf();
}
```

This means that once the media is finished, the service will call stop on itself, which, because of the lifecycle of the service, will trigger Android to call the service's onDestroy method—the perfect place to clean up. Once the cleanup is finished, the service will be deallocated and cease running.

CLEANUP

Cleanup is essential when dealing with media players. If you don't handle this section correctly, a lot of the device's memory can get lost in the shuffle. Here's the onDestroy method where I clean up the media player:

```
@Override
public void onDestroy(){
    super.onDestroy();
    if(mPlayer != null) {
        mPlayer.stop();
        mPlayer.release();
    }
}
```

I must be careful, because an incorrect data source ID or bad media file could leave either of these references null, which would crash the service quite handily when I try to shut them down.

INTERRUPTIONS

When you're writing music software for Android devices, it's vitally important that you remember that the hardware on which your software is running is, in fact, a *phone*. This means you'll need to watch out for several things.

- **Audio focus.** You'll need to use the AudioManager class (introduced in Android 2.2) to register an audio focus listener, because other applications may want to play alerts, navigational directions, or their own horrible music. This is vital to making an Android music playback application play nice with the rest of the system.
- **Controls built into headphones.** You'll want your service to register to receive headset button intents through your manifest (or at runtime when your service is started). At the very least, set up your service to pause when the headset control is clicked.
- **Phone calls.** By watching the phone's call state either through the Telephony Manager or with the audio focus tools, you *absolutely* must watch for incoming phone calls. You must stop all audio when the phone rings. Nothing will enrage your users (and hurt your ratings) more than not accommodating phone calls.

- **Missing SD card.** You'll want to make sure your app handles a missing or removed SD card correctly. Users can mount their external cards as removable drives with the USB cable at any point. Android will alert you if you listen for the `ACTION_MEDIA_REMOVED` intent.

This might seem like a lot of things to look out for (and it is), but never fear, the developers at Google have released an open-source media player (which they ship with the Android source code) that can be a great guide for dealing with this stuff. As always, the documentation will have a lot on the subject as well.

WRAPPING UP

In this chapter, I showed you how to

- Play a simple video
- Play a sound effect when a button is pressed
- Take a previously created service interface and create a functional media player from it

You should now be comfortable with the essentials of media playback. If you're looking to go further with videos (which I hope you are), you'll want to look into using a controller to modify the state of the video view.

Your next step to expand the media playback service is to think about how you'd pass arrays of IDs (playlists) and how you'd deal with updating those playlists on the fly (as users change them).

Android can be a very powerful media platform if you're careful and treat it with care. Go forth and make a crop of better music players—if for no other reason than so I can use them myself.

CHAPTER 9

Determining Locations and Using Maps

One of the chief benefits of building any mobile application is the ability to provide location-aware data to users. Android is no exception. Taking advantage of your user's location to help them make informed decisions should always be in the back of your mind. There is, however, a little to know about the basics of determining and using the device's location. I will show you a few tricks for speedy acquisition and then quickly show you how to display Android's built-in Google Maps view.

LOCATION BASICS

All location information on Android's systems is reached through Android's Location Manager class. There is, as you might have guessed, a permission requirement before you can access the user's location field.

MOTHER MAY I?

If you want to get the location of a user's device, you'll need to add the location permission to your manifest. Depending on the level of location data you want to acquire, you'll need to declare one of the following permissions:

```
<uses-permission
    android:name="android.permission.ACCESS_COARSE_LOCATION"/>
<uses-permission
    android:name="android.permission.ACCESS_FINE_LOCATION" />
```

The `<uses-permission>` tag should be declared inside the manifest but outside the `<application>` section.

BE CAREFUL WHAT YOU ASK FOR

Some users, bless their paranoid cotton socks, pay very close attention to the permissions you request in your manifest (each permission generates a warning when the app is purchased or downloaded from Google Play). Several high-profile applications have been hit by negative reviews and user outrage for adding a location permission that didn't make sense. If you're going to use the location services on the device, make sure it's for the direct benefit of your users. Do otherwise, and your users *will* find out. Further, it's always a good idea to have a webpage that explains each permission you use. Those who care about it will find their way to it—and if they're informed, they will be less likely to complain.

FINDING A GOOD SUPPLIER

Your first step in using the location service, after you've added the permission of course, is finding a good supplier. Each device could have several different location services beyond the time- and power-consuming GPS system. Android allows you to specify criteria for the eventual provider you'll use. You do this by building a list of features you'd like and then asking Android for the one that best suits your needs. Here's a rather idealistic example I've put together using the getBestProvider method:

```
public static String getBestProvider(LocationManager locationManager){
    Criteria criteria = new Criteria();
    criteria.setAccuracy(Criteria.ACCURACY_COARSE);
    criteria.setPowerRequirement(Criteria.POWER_LOW);
```

```
    criteria.setCostAllowed(false);
return locationManager.getBestProvider(criteria, true);
}
```

Before calling the getBestProvider method, you'll need to obtain a LocationManager object, which you can do with the following code:

```
LocationManager mLocationManager;

@Override
public void onCreate(Bundle savedInstanceState) {
   super.onCreate(savedInstanceState);
   setContentView(R.layout.activity_main);

   mLocationManager = (LocationManager)
      getSystemService(Context.LOCATION_SERVICE);
}
```

Typically, I'll stash this reference away somewhere so I never have to find it again.

GETTING THE GOODS

Once you've received the string ID for your ideal provider, you can register and start receiving location updates from the provider. Here's the code to register for updates using the getBestProvider function that we wrote earlier:

```
@Override
public void onCreate(Bundle savedInstanceState) {
   super.onCreate(savedInstanceState);
   setContentView(R.layout.activity_main);

   mLocationManager = (LocationManager)
      getSystemService(Context.LOCATION_SERVICE);

   String provider = getBestProvider(mLocationManager);
   mLocationManager.requestLocationUpdates(
      provider, 60000, 100, this);
}
```

Calling this requestLocationUpdates method will result in the onLocationChanged method being invoked every time the user's location is changed according to the criteria you set. Along with the provider string, you'll need to tell the system the minimum time between updates (in my case, 60 seconds—the documentation suggests not having it poll any faster than that), the minimum distance between intervals (in my case, 1000 meters), and the object that implements the LocationListener interface you want to receive call-backs. Here are the methods you're required to override:

```
public void onLocationChanged(final Location location) {}
@Override
public void onProviderDisabled(String provider) {}
@Override
public void onProviderEnabled(String provider) {}
@Override
public void onStatusChanged(String provider, int status, Bundle extras) {}
```

The method I'm most interested in, in this case, is the onLocationChanged method. It will pass me that all-important location object. With that data, I can then call getLatitude and getLongitude. And with that, I know—with as much accuracy as possible—where in the world the device is.

Further, the LocationManager object contains an important static helper method named distanceBetween, which will calculate the distance between geographic points. I point out this helper because I find myself using it all the time.

THE SNEAKY SHORTCUT

It can sometimes take many seconds for the location manager to spit out a user's location. There's a solution you can take advantage of to at least display an old value while the real location is being determined. You can, either before or after registering your listener, call getLastKnownLocation on your location manager using the provider you want.

```
mLocationManager.getLastKnownLocation(provider);
```

This can provide some interesting results (especially if the device has spent a long time aloft in an airplane without an Internet connection), but it can often give the user something to look at or laugh at while you find their real location. To use this trick, you must define the android.permission.ACCESS_FINE_LOCATION permission.

THAT'S IT!

As much as I would like to say that this is an incredibly complex operation, it's about as hard as tying your shoelaces. Given what you've been through up to this point, getting the location from the LocationManager should be a cakewalk. That said, I had my fair share of issues in writing the code for this chapter. If you are stumped, check the documentation and press on!

SHOW ME THE MAP!

FIGURE 9.1 This is how your Android settings should look.

Determining your user's location is one thing, but actually putting those two indecipherable numbers (longitude and latitude) into context is where software gets a little more complex. Interestingly enough, the configuration needed to get a map onscreen is far more complex than the code to manipulate it. If you want to follow along, go ahead and create a new Android project.

BEFORE WE GET STARTED

The Google Maps SDK gives us a component named `MapFragment`. Even though we haven't covered fragments before, I'm confident that you can handle it! I am going to cover fragments in depth in the next chapter, so now is a great time to briefly see them in action before you learn exactly how they work.

GETTING THE LIBRARY

The `MapFragment` component is available only in the Google Play Services API, which is a superset of the Android SDK. To use these APIs, you'll need to download the Play Services library using the SDK manager (the same way you got the Ice Cream Sandwich and Gingerbread SDKs back in Chapter 1). **Figure 9.1** shows what SDK manager options you'll want to download.

FIGURE 9.2
Your Eclipse Android
project settings

If you haven't done so already, also grab the Android Support Repository, the Android Support Library, and the Google Repository. Your IDE will use these pieces for the rest of the projects covered in this book, so it's a good idea to grab them now.

Our IDEs are going to slightly diverge in the setup for this project, but the code will ultimately be the same.

ECLIPSE

Create a new project in Eclipse. After it's created, right-click the project and select Properties. In the Properties dialog, look for Android on the left. In the Android menu, select the Google API that corresponds with the version of Android you're targeting. To make it easy, select the Google APIs for 4.3. **Figure 9.2** shows what your settings should look like.

ANDROID STUDIO

Android Studio is a little more complicated, but also a little more exciting. This will be our first foray into adding a property to the Gradle build file. I won't go into all the details of the contents of the build file yet; I'll cover that in depth in Chapter 13.

Open your project's inner Gradle file. In the example code, this is located in `MapsDemo Project/MapsDemo/build.gradle`; in your code it should be in the same location.

In this file, look for two sections called dependencies. In the second dependencies section, add the following highlighted line:

```
dependencies {
    compile 'com.android.support:appcompat-v7:18.0.0'
    compile 'com.google.android.gms:play-services:3.2.25'
}
```

Now that the Gradle file has a new dependency, sync the Gradle file with your project by selecting Tools > Android > Sync Project with Gradle Files. Then rebuild by selecting Build > Rebuild.

That's it! The libraries are now added to your project.

Once you've set up your SDK values correctly, there are a few things in the manifest I need to talk with you about.

ADDING TO THE MANIFEST

There are a few critical things that, through the manifest, you need to tell the system.

```
<manifest> <!--Rest of the manifest omitted here for brevity.-->
    ...
    <uses-permission android:name="com.google.android.providers.gsf.permission.
    → READ_GSERVICES">
    <uses-permission android:name="android.permission.INTERNET"/>
    <uses-permission android:name="android.permission.ACCESS_NETWORK_STATE"/>
    <uses-permission android:name="android.permission.WRITE_EXTERNAL_STORAGE"/>


    <application>
    ...
    </application>
</manifest>
```

- Even if you can compile, the application will crash unless you explicitly have permission to use Play services.
- The MapFragment will download its map from the network, so it needs to be able to access the Internet.
- The MapFragment also needs access to the network state as an optimization to better recover from gaining network connectivity. This, unfortunately, is not optional.
- The MapFragment needs the ability to write to external storage. All the map tiles that it downloads will be saved into an external storage cache to speed up future requests and cut down on data usage.

Now, with that out of the way, it's time to start playing with some maps!

ADJUSTING THE ACTIVITY

Using the MapFragment is surprisingly simple, and it only requires making a couple of small modifications to your base project. The first is to change your Activity class to a FragmentActivity:

```java
public class MapsExampleProjectActivity extends FragmentActivity {
  @Override
  public void onCreate(Bundle savedInstanceState) {
    super.onCreate(savedInstanceState);
    setContentView(R.layout.activity_main);
  }
}
```

A FragmentActivity means that this activity is going to be used to manage fragments—in our case, a MapFragment. Now that you have your Activity class switched over to the FragmentActivity class, you can add the MapFragment to your activity_main.xml layout file.

CREATING A MAPFRAGMENT

This is where Android will draw its map tiles. It basically behaves exactly like any other view, except it is using a fragment tag instead of an ImageView or a TextView.

Here's what my simple activity_main.xml file looks like right now:

```xml
<?xml version="1.0" encoding="utf-8"?>
<RelativeLayout xmlns:android="http://schemas.android.com/apk/res/android"
  android:layout_width="match_parent"
  android:layout_height="match_parent">

  <fragment
    android:id="@+id/map_fragment"
    class="com.google.android.gms.maps.SupportMapFragment"
    android:layout_width="match_parent"
    android:layout_height="match_parent" />

</RelativeLayout>
```

As you can see, I've placed my MapFragment as the only thing onscreen. You can actually place it anywhere you want, just as you would position any other view. Further, it doesn't require, as the ListActivity does, a special reserved Android ID.

FIGURE 9.3 Without an API key, your application cannot receive any map data from the Google Maps servers.

You should be able to run your project now—hooray! But there's one small problem. Everything is gray, and there are no maps (**Figure 9.3**). We have zoom buttons, but where is the globe? This is what your maps will look like if there was a problem connecting with the Google Maps servers, which most likely is indicative of an error in your API key. Where do you get a maps API key? I'm so glad you asked.

GOOGLE MAPS API KEY

Google is nice and all, but it doesn't just give away map API calls for free. Well, technically it does, since an API key doesn't cost you any money, but you still need to sign up for one.

SIGNING UP FOR A MAP KEY

Getting a map key isn't as easy as it could be, but I'm going to give you a few pointers to help you make it through the process.

1. Go to https://code.google.com/apis/console and sign in with your Google account. From there, follow the instructions to create a new API project.

FIGURE 9.4 Turn on the toggle for Google Maps Android API v2.

⬡ Google Compute Engine	⑦	OFF
✉ Google Contacts CardDAV API	⑦	OFF
📱 Google Maps Android API v2	⑦	ON
📍 Google Maps API v2	⑦	OFF
📍 Google Maps API v3	⑦	OFF

Once you've created your new API project, you should see a long list of toggle switches, as in **Figure 9.4**. About halfway down the list is a toggle for Google Maps Android API v2. That's the switch you want.

2. Go ahead and turn it on.

3. On the left menu, select the API Access page. At the bottom of the API access page, you will see a section named Simple API Access, and a button right below labeled Create New Android Key. As you can imagine, this is where we are going to get the key!

4. Click the Create New Android Key button and take a look at the dialog. It's asking for a string of characters that contains the SHA (Secure Hash Algorithm) of your signing key, and the name of your application package. This sounds complicated, but it's easy.

5. Open a Terminal window, type the following into the command line, and press Enter:

   `keytool -list -keystore ~/.android/debug.keystore`

   It should then prompt you for a password. The default debug keystore password is android, but it's not required, and you can just press Enter and still get the information you need.

   What you're looking for is all the characters printed after `Certificate fingerprint (SHA1):`.

6. Enter the string that displays into the dialog.

7. After that, append a colon (:) followed by your application's package name. For the example code, it looks like this:

   `54:1B:29:89:9A:87:36:43:GG:LL:92:26:5A:42:64:com.peachpit.mapsdemo`

   (This SHA has been shortened and changed for brevity.)

   This will generate an API key that will work specifically while debugging. When you release your application to the market, you will have to do this again for a new key, but we will cover that in Chapter 12.

8. Click OK.

Whew, we did it. Generating API keys is never fun, and it's always easy to run into trouble. If you have any issues, try checking out https://developers.google.com/maps/documentation/android. There's lots of great information there that will help you troubleshoot any problems you run into.

USING YOUR MAPS API KEY

The last piece of the puzzle is to put your API key into your application. Open your Android Manifest file, and make a new entry for the API key metadata within the application tag:

```
<manifest><!--Rest of the manifest omitted here for brevity.-->
.  <application>
      <meta-data
         android:name="com.google.android.maps.v2.API_KEY"
         android:value="Your api key"/>
.  </application>
</manifest>
```

RUN, BABY, RUN

You've configured everything, dotted all your i's, and crossed all your t's. It's time to take this map view out for a spin. When it comes time to move and render the map, you'll primarily be interfacing with `CameraUpdates` and `MarkerOptions`. With these two pieces, you can accomplish a lot of amazing things and leverage all the work that Google has already done for you. The simple work for my example is all done in my sample code's onCreate method:

```
@Override
protected void onCreate(Bundle savedInstanceState) {
    super.onCreate(savedInstanceState);
    setContentView(R.layout.activity_main);

    SupportMapFragment fragment = (SupportMapFragment)
       getSupportFragmentManager().findFragmentById(
          R.id.map_fragment);

    // A position on the globe
    LatLng latLng = new LatLng(40.734641, -73.996181);

    // the desired zoom level, in the range of 2.0 to 21.0
    // 2.0 being all the way out and 21.0 being all the way in
    float zoomLevel = 10.0f;
    CameraUpdate cameraUpdate =
       CameraUpdateFactory.newLatLngZoom(latLng, zoomLevel);
    fragment.getMap().animateCamera(cameraUpdate);
```

FIGURE 9.5 New York City. The biggest small town you'll ever know.

```
// Marker options are how we can get markers onto the map
MarkerOptions marker = new MarkerOptions();
marker.position(latLng);
fragment.getMap().addMarker(marker);
}
```

In this code, I'm doing a few important things:

1. Retrieving the MapView from my layout with the inimitable findViewById method.

2. Obtaining a reference to my MapFragment.

3. Creating a new LatLng on which to center the map.

4. Panning and zooming the camera to the desired location.

5. Dropping a marker on the location that we are moving toward.

The location listed in the example happens to be New York City (where I'm currently writing this book), and I've set the zoom level high enough that you can almost see my house—all right, maybe not! **Figure 9.5** shows what all your hard work thus far has yielded.

WRAPPING UP

In this chapter, I showed you the very basics for finding a device's location and displaying a map onscreen. As always, be very careful what kind of location services you use, especially while the user is not in your application. Nothing will drain a user's battery faster—and make them angrier—than heavy locational lookups in the background. If you're planning a very location-heavy application, be sure to do *lots* of battery-draw testing before you release it. Your users and your application's ratings will be much happier for it.

CHAPTER 10

Tablets, Fragments, and Action Bars, Oh My

So we've made it this far, and we've barely talked about fragments at all. Well, there's reason behind this madness, I assure you. Fragments were added to the framework at a time when the Android platform was evolving to accommodate larger screens and needed a strategy for allowing developers to design one application to work across a myriad of devices.

Around the same time, the action bar was added to the framework. The action bar is a window feature that aims to provide a consistent navigation and action pattern for Android applications. Much like the menu bar across the top of all screens in OS X and the menu functionality tied to the top of each application window in Windows, the action bar serves as a universal (but styleable) design that users are accustomed to and have come to expect.

FRAGMENTS

Fragments, conceptually, are like activities with a slightly more complex lifecycle. They can be given a screen to themselves if there isn't much room, or they can be placed with many other fragments on a larger tablet screen. An activity can contain any number of fragments. In this way, the Android SDK allows you to expand and collapse the views in your application to take advantage of more and less screen space. There is one thing the activity can do that the fragment cannot—the activity can register for intents in the manifest; fragments rely on their host activity to pass on launch information. Further, it's important to implement fragments such that they are totally unaware of what other fragments are visible. This becomes important, because you'll want to change that configuration depending on how much space you have.

If you're planning on coding along with me in this chapter, make sure you have a project that is set to version 3.0 or higher of the Android SDK (API Level 11 or greater).

THE LIFECYCLE OF THE FRAGMENT

Fragments have fairly complex lifecycles. There are many methods to explore, but the onCreate View method must be implemented for the fragment to appear onscreen. onCreateView is your fragment's one chance to create a view to display onscreen. If you fail to return a view to the system, your application will crash and burn.

Here is the startup lifecycle; the methods are listed in the order the system will call them:

- onAttach is called when your fragment is attaching to an activity.
- onCreate is called when the fragment is being initialized. This is a great place to initialize any variables you'll need later.
- onCreateView is your opportunity to create and return the fragment's root view. This is the first method that will be called if your fragment is returning to the screen after having been previously paused.
- onStart is similar to the same call on the activity; it is called when the fragment is about to be placed onscreen.
- onResume is called when the fragment is back onscreen.

At this point, your fragment is frolicking on the screen, receiving touch and key events, or just hanging around and looking great. If the user leaves the screen or switches to a view that no longer includes the fragment, the following shutdown lifecycle will occur:

- onPause is called if the fragment is removed from the screen or the user presses the home button. This is the only part of the shutdown lifecycle you're guaranteed to get (it would be the only method you get in the rare situation that your application is put in the background and then your process is killed due to resource constraints). onPause is the best time for you to save any data or state information that you want the user to be able to see when the fragment is resumed later.
- onStop is similar to the activity's version of this method; it is called when your fragment has left the screen. It tends to be called in conjunction with the activity's onStop method.

- `onDestroyView` is your last chance to pull data out of the views before they go away.

- `onDestroy` is called when the fragment is being removed from the screen and will not return. This is the time to make sure all your threads are stopped, loaders are canceled, and any broadcast receivers are unregistered.

- `onDetach` is called as the fragment loses its association with an activity; it is the last of your methods the system will call before the fragment heads to the great garbage collector in the sky.

CREATING A FRAGMENT

To create a fragment, you'll need to create a Java class that extends the `Fragment` class. An incredibly simple implementation would look something like this:

```java
public class ContentFragment extends Fragment{
    @Override
    public View onCreateView(LayoutInflater inflater,
        ViewGroup container, Bundle savedInstanceState) {
        View root = inflater.inflate(R.layout.fragment_content,
            container, false);
        ...
        return root;
    }
}
```

Fragments, of course, need their own layouts to show anything onscreen. The `Content Fragment` class in the sample implementation will show a simple text view. Here is the `fragment_content.xml` file whose contents will be drawn as the fragment itself:

```xml
<?xml version="1.0" encoding="utf-8"?>
<RelativeLayout xmlns:android="http://schemas.android.com/apk/res/android"
    android:layout_width="match_parent"
    android:layout_height="match_parent">

    <TextView
        android:id="@+id/header_text"
        android:layout_width="wrap_content"
        android:layout_height="wrap_content"
        android:text="@string/hello_world" />

    <TextView
        android:id="@+id/content_text "
        android:layout_width="wrap_content"
```

```
        android:layout_height="wrap_content"
        android:text="@string/lorem_ipsum" />
```

```
</RelativeLayout>
```

With the XML layout file and the new ContentFragment class, you'll have a very basic but functional fragment for displaying text on the screen. Just as with using an activity, you can call findViewById on the root view from onCreateView:

```
TextView mContentTextView;
@Override
public View onCreateView(LayoutInflater inflater,
   ViewGroup container, Bundle savedInstanceState) {
   View root = inflater.inflate(R.layout.fragment_content,
      container, false);
   TextView tv =
      (TextView) root.findViewById (R.id.header_text);
   tv.setText("Checking out fragments!");
   mContentTextView = (TextView) root.findViewById(R.id.content_text);
   return root;
}
```

If you need to access the root view outside of onCreateView, you can safely save it in a member variable, or you can call the getView method, which will return the view that was returned from onCreateView. Here's what a method accessing getView might look like:

```
private void setContentText(String text){
   TextView tv =
      (TextView) getView().findViewById (R.id.content_text);
   tv.setText(text);
}
```

Keep in mind, however, that the getView method works only after you've returned from onCreateView. While you now have a fully functioning fragment, you still need to make it appear onscreen.

SHOWING A FRAGMENT

There are two main ways you can make fragments appear onscreen.

USING XML
You can declare a fragment in an XML layout to make the fragment appear onscreen, like so:

```
File: res/layout/activity_main.xml
<?xml version="1.0" encoding="utf-8"?>
```

FIGURE 10.1 A fragment with a single text view

```xml
<LinearLayout xmlns:android="http://schemas.android.com/apk/res/android"
    android:layout_width="match_parent"
    android:layout_height="match_parent">

    <fragment
        android:id="@+id/list_fragment"
        android:name="com.peachpit.fragmentdemo.ContentFragment"
        android:layout_width="match_parent"
        android:layout_height="match_parent" />
</LinearLayout>
```

This layout can then be set as the content view for a FragmentActivity, just like any other layout file:

```java
public class ContentViewingActivity extends FragmentActivity{
    public void onCreate(Bundle data){
        super.onCreate(data);
        setContentView(R.layout.activity_main);
    }
}
```

Figure 10.1 shows the results of using XML to make the fragment appear onscreen.

Fragments, when set up this way, can be placed onscreen the same way as views, which
makes it easy to include many of them in a single layout file. So if one fragment is awesome, two fragments must be even more awesome! Let's create another fragment, and call it
DemoListFragment.

```java
public class DemoListFragment extends ListFragment {
  @Override
  public void onCreate(Bundle savedInstanceState) {
    super.onCreate(savedInstanceState);
    ArrayList<String> data = new ArrayList<String>();
    for(int i = 0; i < 20; i++){
      data.add("Item " + i);
    }
    ArrayAdapter<String> adapter =
      new ArrayAdapter<String>(getActivity(),
        android.R.layout.simple_list_item_1, data);
    setListAdapter(adapter);
  }
}
```

A list fragment is very similar to the ListActivity we covered in Chapter 5, except that
it's a fragment. It has a ListView built into it, and if you want to override the default list in it,
you just inflate a layout file that contains a ListView that has an ID of android.R.id.list.
But since we aren't inflating a custom layout here, it's OK to do all the fragment setup logic in
onCreate.

Now that we have two fragments, let's set this list fragment to show only while the device
is in landscape. In your project, create a new folder in the res/ folder and name it layout-
land. Into that new folder, put a new XML file named activity_main.xml (exactly the same
as in the res/layout folder). As we know from Chapter 7, when the device is in landscape,
it will choose this file instead of the default one. Go ahead and add this XML to the layout (it
shows a ListFragment with the ContentFragment next to it):

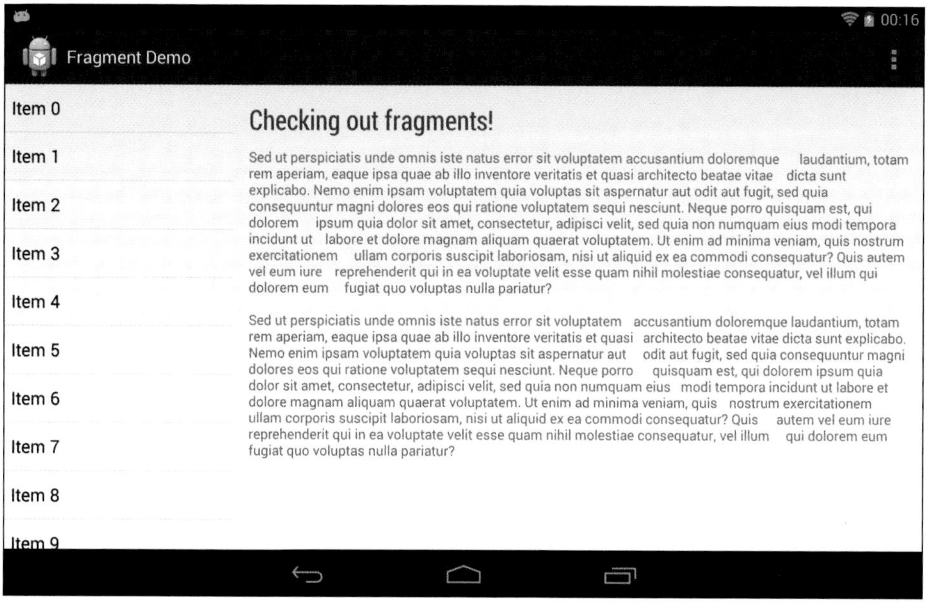

FIGURE 10.2 Two fragments on one screen

```xml
<?xml version="1.0" encoding="utf-8"?>
<LinearLayout xmlns:android="http://schemas.android.com/apk/res/android"
    android:layout_width="match_parent"
    android:layout_height="match_parent"
    android:orientation="horizontal" >
    <fragment
        android:id="@+id/list_fragment"
        android:name="com.peachpit.fragments.DemoListFragment"
        android:layout_width="0dp"
        android:layout_height="match_parent"
        android:layout_weight="1"/>
    <fragment
        android:id="@+id/content_fragment"
        android:name="com. peachpit.fragments.ContentFragment"
        android:layout_width="0dp"
        android:layout_height="match_parent"
        android:layout_weight="3"/>
</LinearLayout>
```

I've used a linear layout and some weighting in the fragments to give the DemoList Fragment the left one-third of the screen and the ContentFragment the right two-thirds. (If you're wondering about DemoListFragment, you can find it in the sample code for this chapter.)

Figure 10.2 shows what it looks like on a device in landscape mode.

USING THE FRAGMENT MANAGER

Although being able to lay out fragments in the XML files is great, you'll want to be able to interact with the fragments on your screen at runtime as well. For this, you'll use the FragmentManager, which is Android's tool for manipulating fragments.

Getting a fragment manager on Honeycomb and later requires you to call getFragment Manager. Getting a fragment manager for earlier devices requires you to call getSupport FragmentManager from a FragmentActivity.

You can add fragments to the screen programmatically with the following code:

```
FragmentManager manager = getSupportFragmentManager();
FragmentTransaction ft = manager.beginTransaction();
ft.add(containerViewId, new DemoListFragment());
ft.commit();
```

The variable containerViewId should refer to an existing ViewGroup in your activity's layout where the new fragment should be placed. You can also, at a later time, replace one fragment with another by calling replace(containerViewId, newFragment);, where containerViewId specifies the view container that currently holds the fragment you'd like to replace. You can replace only fragments that were previously added using a FragmentManager transaction; fragments declared statically in XML layouts cannot be replaced.

By using either XML or the fragment manager to set up and modify your fragments, you should have no trouble building complex, scalable, and beautiful applications that render well on both handsets and tablets.

Remember that all fragments should work independently of their siblings (in much the same way that activities should stay independent), even if they might share the same screen.

Given the power of Android's layout folders (which we covered at length in Chapters 3 and 7), you should see the possibilities in building one layout for tablets (which could have several fragments on it) and building another for small-screened phones (which would have only one visible fragment at a time).

If you're looking for a simple example, I highly recommend you take a look at the project in the sample code for this chapter.

PROVIDING BACKWARD COMPATIBILITY

Android has, thankfully, bundled fragments into its compatibility library. This means you can work with fragments even if you're planning on supporting pre-3.0 devices. I highly recommend that you use it whenever you can. In Eclipse, installing it is as simple as selecting the menu item shown in **Figure 10.3**.

In Android studio, all you have to do is add the following line to the second dependencies section of your Gradle file (the one that doesn't have classpath 'com.android.tools. build:gradle:0.X.+' in it). If there isn't a second dependencies section, go ahead and add it.

```
dependencies {
    compile 'com.android.support:support-v4:18.0.0'
}
```

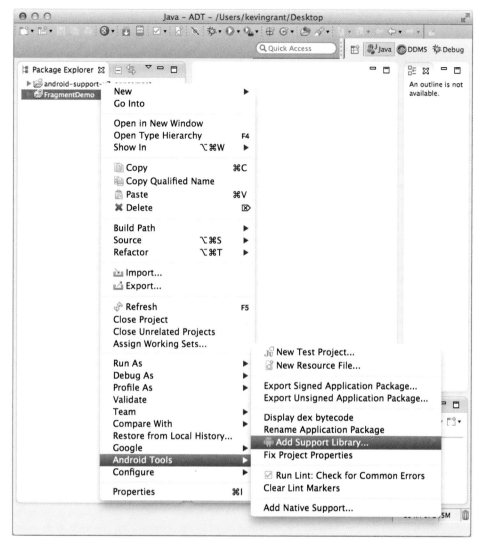

FIGURE 10.3
Installing the compatibility library

Take note, however, that building your project against a 3.0 or higher version and still using the compatibility libraries at the same time can get a little complicated. If you're doing this, make sure all your imports come from the support library like this:

```
import android.support.v4.app.Fragment;
```

instead of like this:

```
import android.app.Fragment;
```

Using the support library will ensure that your application will run correctly on newer and older systems alike.

Further, if you're planning on using the compatibility library and fragments, remember that you'll need to use a `FragmentActivity` instead of a regular activity; or, as you will see in the next section, you can also use an `ActionBarActivity`.

With the compatibility support and the dynamic nature of fragments, it becomes quite possible to create an application with a great interaction model that works well on both phones and tablets. I don't have the space to spell it all out here, but there is sample code for achieving this in the companion source code for this chapter. Remember what you've read here, and take a look through it.

THE ACTION BAR

With the transition from Android 2.3 to 3.0, Google eliminated both the search button and the menu key. From personal experience, I can tell you that many new users never find functionality that is placed in the options menu. Its removal from the system is, indeed, a very good thing.

Google moved the icons that used to reside in the options menu to the action bar. Further, you can specify a search view in the action bar (to replace the search button). This takes up more screen space, but on a tablet (and on later phones), there is more than enough space to go around.

The action bar now represents the primary way your users will navigate through your applications. Sadly, this tool is available only to versions 3.0 (target 11) or later, but it is available to earlier versions if you use the AppCompat library. Since there is a decent chance you will want to know how to get this support action bar working, and since the APIs for the support action bar and the actual action bar are nearly identical, I'll quickly show you how in both Eclipse and Android Studio before going on.

SETTING UP THE APPCOMPAT LIBRARY

If you really aren't interested in supporting Android versions prior to 3.0, set your project's target Android version to 11 and skip ahead to the section "Adding Elements to the Action Bar." Those of you who are choosing to support all devices, carry on.

Android Studio wins the award for ease of setup with the AppCompat library. In your project's Gradle file, add this highlighted line in the same place that the support library is located:

```
dependencies {
    compile 'com.android.support:support-v4:18.0.0'
    compile 'com.android.support:appcompat-v7:18.0.0'
}
```

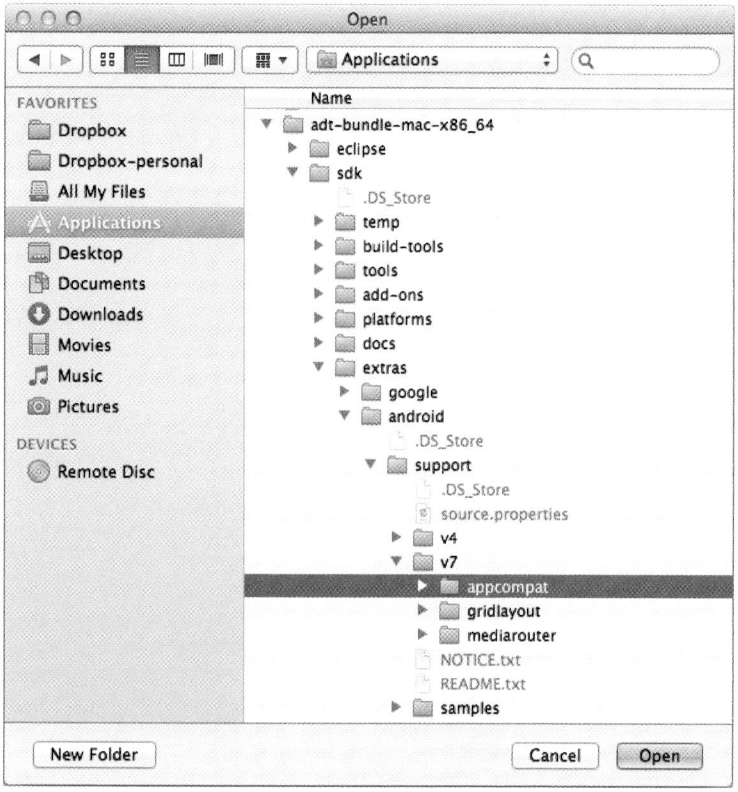

FIGURE 10.4 Locate the AppCompat library in your SDK.

All done! Just select Tools > Android > Sync Project With Gradle Files to have Android Studio pull this library into your project.

On Eclipse, it will take a little more elbow grease, but it's still pretty easy. The first thing you need to verify is that you have downloaded the support repository. This is located in the SDK Manager (Window > Android SDK Manager). At the bottom of the list, look for the Android Support Repository, and download it if you haven't already.

Now, with your SDK ready, you need to import the AppCompat project as an Android library. This is almost identical to how you have been importing the sample code for this book into Eclipse. Select File > Import, and then locate where you have Eclipse ADT installed. Within the installation folder, choose sdk > extras > android > support > v7 > appcompat, and click OK (**Figure 10.4**). If you don't see the appcompat file there, head back to the SDK Manager and download the support repository again.

The AppCompat library is now in your Eclipse workspace, which allows you to add this project onto other projects to provide its functionality. Now create a new project, and leave the minimum SDK at 8 or 9 (if you've downloaded them; otherwise, just set it to the lowest version you have). With your new project created, we are going to add the AppCompat library to it.

FIGURE 10.5 Adding appcompat as a library project

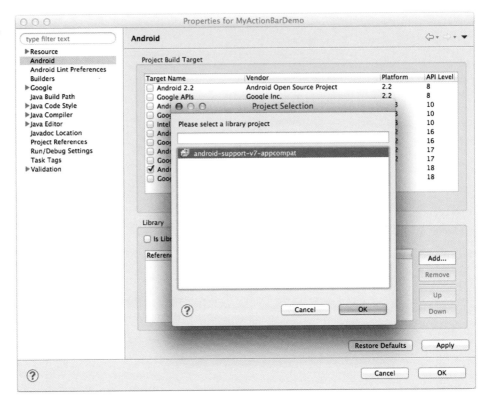

Right-click your new project folder in Eclipse, and select Properties from the bottom of the menu. From the left menu in the Properties dialog, select Android. On the right, below the Project Build Target section, is the section where you can add Android libraries. Click Add, and a dialog with a list of possible Android libraries in your workspace will appear. Select android-support-v7-compat, and click OK (**Figure 10.5**).

Now look at the far left menu again, and select Java Build Path. On the right, you should see four tabs. Select the third tab, Libraries, and then click Add JARs. Navigate into the AppCompat library project and look in the `libs` folder for the file `appcompat.jar` (**Figure 10.6**). Select it, and click OK. Lastly, select the Order and Export tab, and select the `appcompat.jar` file (**Figure 10.7**). You're all set! Now click OK to apply the changes and return to the project.

Assuming everything worked as planned, select Project > Clean > Clean All Projects, and click OK to force Eclipse to rebuild the workspace and make sure that your libraries are playing nicely with each other.

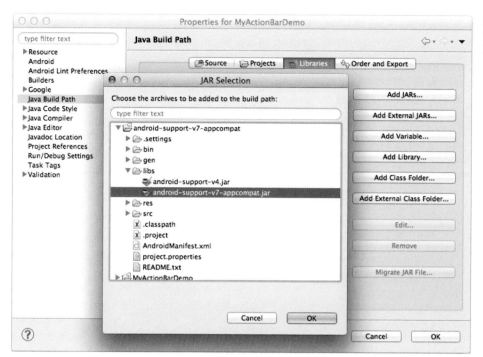

FIGURE 10.6 Adding
appcompat.jar to your
project's build path

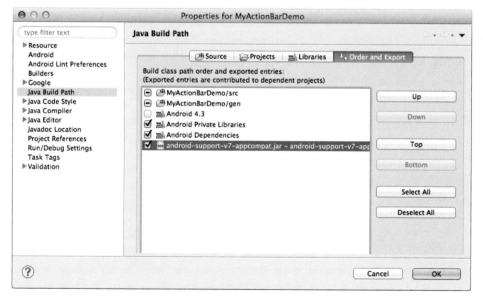

FIGURE 10.7 Enable
appcompat in the
Order and Export tab.

SHOWING THE ACTION BAR

Now there are only two pieces left to showing the action bar. The first is straightforward. In the MainActivity that was created with your project, change extends Activity to extends ActionBarActivity. This might require you to organize (Eclipse) or optimize (Android Studio) imports to get your IDE to recognize the new class. The app should compile, and it looks like you're on your way to glory. But if you run this code, you will be prompted with an error. Look in the logs, and you'll see this error:

```
java.lang.IllegalStateException: You need to use a Theme.AppCompat theme
→ (or descendant) with this activity.
```

Often, logs can be meaningless or hard to decipher. This, however, is not one of those times. As it suggests, we need to go into our styles.xml file and modify the theme for our application. Open styles.xml (res/values/styles.xml) and change

```
<style name="AppBaseTheme" parent="android:Theme.Light">
```

to

```
<style name="AppBaseTheme" parent="Theme.AppCompat.Light">
```

While we're at it, we also should modify the styles.xml in all the other resource folders. The app creation wizard usually creates a similar styles.xml file in res/values-v11 and res/values-v14. Apply this same change to those styles, and try running your application again. If you're running your application on an emulator that's 4.0 and above, congratulations, it looks exactly like all the other examples in this book! Don't roll your eyes so quickly—the power of AppCompat is that now, if you run this application on a device running Android 2.2 Froyo or Android 2.3 Gingerbread, it will look nearly identical. Now that's awesome.

ADDING ELEMENTS TO THE ACTION BAR

Now that we have our action bar set up and running for all desired versions, let's get into the fun stuff. In addition to allowing you to set your own title with a call to setTitle, the action bar can handle three different types of objects:

- Menu items, both in a drop-down menu on the right side and as actionable items in the bar itself.
- Tabs. Buttons along the top, built to manipulate fragments on the screen.
- Action views. Search boxes and drop-down lists (for things like sort orders, account selection, or death-ray intensities).

Further, Android will always make your application icon (farthest to the left) clickable. It is expected that tapping this icon will, by default, return the user to your application's home screen (whatever this means to your application's behavior). You can also visually indicate that the home icon will go one level back in the activity stack by calling setDisplay HomeAsUpEnabled(true).

FIGURE 10.8 Adding an action bar menu item

The way you make changes to what's in the action bar is very similar to how you used to interact with the options menu. This is not by accident. Because the action bar is supposed to replace the options menu, you call methods and configure files similarly to how you used to deal with the menu. This also makes it easy to gracefully degrade service to phones on older versions of the Android SDK.

ADDING A MENU ITEM

Action bar menu items are actionable items that are visible on the right side of your action bar (**Figure 10.8**). They are placed there by overriding onCreateOptionsMenu in your activity and adding the menu items you'd like. By default, the new project wizard generates the code that overrides this function for you. Let's take a look into the menu.xml file that's being inflated and try to add our own menu item.

Here's the code, located in your ActionBarActivity (or Activity), that is inflating the menu into the action bar:

```
@Override
public boolean onCreateOptionsMenu(Menu menu) {
    // Inflate the menu; this adds items to the ActionBar if it is present.
    getMenuInflater().inflate(R.menu.main, menu);
    return true;
}
```

And here is what the XML code for a basic action bar menu item looks like:

```
<menu xmlns:android="http://schemas.android.com/apk/res/android"
    xmlns:app="http://schemas.android.com/apk/res-auto">
    <item
        android:id="@+id/action_add_item"
        android:title="@string/action_add_item"
        android:icon="@drawable/ic_menu_add"
        android:orderInCategory="100"
        android:showAsAction="always"
        app:showAsAction="always" />
</menu>
```

Let's dissect what's going on here. The first block is fairly unambiguous. We are getting the menu inflater, and inflating the layout file referenced by R.menu.main. All menu XML files should be located in the res/menu/ folder, kept separate from your other layout files.

The XML file is a little more interesting. The first line should seem familiar. This is the ID of the menu item. Just like a regular view, this menu item will be referenced by the ID given in this file. The title is a multipurpose piece of text that is used by the system in a number of ways. If the item is just text, you will see this title. If the menu item gets pushed into the action overflow, you will see this title there. Finally, if you have the item showing only the icon and no text, the user will be shown this text in a pop-up when long-pressing the button, letting them know what this is. orderInCategory sets the importance of this menu item, such that it will be shown earlier or later in the ordering depending on its value. In this case, the lower the number, the higher the priority.

The last and possibly most interesting piece here is the showAsAction attribute. We have it set to always, but you can change it to ifRoom, withText, never, or any combination of them by adding the pipe (|) character. For example, if you want to show a menu item always and with the text, you would set it to always|withText. The next interesting thing about this menu item is that we are duplicating showAsAction with the app prefix instead of the Android prefix. Because of how the AppCompat action bar is implemented, it is necessary to add this twice: once for the default action bar implementation, and once for the AppCompat implementation. It isn't the most ideal scenario, but it's still a far more practical solution than trying to implement a custom menu solution yourself.

TIP: When trying to figure out what arguments an XML item can take, press Control+spacebar to get a drop-down list of all possible arguments for that item.

REACTING TO MENU ITEM CLICKS

When the user clicks one of your action bar menu items, Android will call your implementation of the onOptionsItemSelected method. Here's my very simple example method:

```
public boolean onOptionsItemSelected(MenuItem item){
    int id = item.getItemId();
    if(id == android.R.id.home){
        // The user clicked the left-hand app icon.
        // As this is the home screen, ignore it.
        return true;
    } else if (id == R.id.action_settings) {
        // Launch the settings
        return true;
    }
    // Return false if you didn't handle this id
    return false;
}
```

With that, you should have the basics of creating both options menu and action bar menu items. If you desire, you can also create menu options dynamically by adding them in the onCreateOptionsMenu. While it's not as elegant, sometimes it's the only way to get the job done.

```
@Override
public boolean onCreateOptionsMenu(Menu menu) {
    int groupId = -1; // No group for this one
    int itemId = 123456; // TODO Generate a better ID somewhere
    int order = 100;
    menu.add(groupId, itemId, order, "Settings");
    return true;
}
```

ADDING A TAB

Placing a tab in the action bar is a totally different process. You'll use the ActionBar class itself to add a tab. Further, you'll need to implement an ActionBar.TabListener onto your activity (it tells the system, through a series of overridden methods, what to do when the tab is tapped by the user).

Once you've implemented your listener, you should then add the following code to your activity's onCreate method:

```
@Override
protected void onCreate(Bundle savedInstanceState) {
    super.onCreate(savedInstanceState);
    setContentView(R.layout.activity_main);

    ActionBar bar = getSupportActionBar();
    // Use getActionBar() if not using AppCompat lib

    bar.setNavigationMode(ActionBar.NAVIGATION_MODE_TABS);
    ActionBar.Tab tab1 = bar.newTab();
    tab1.setText("Tab Text");
    tab1.setTabListener(new ExampleTabListener());
    bar.addTab(tab1);
}
```

FIGURE 10.9

Adding tabs under the
action bar

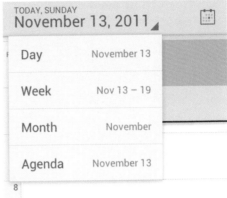

FIGURE 10.10 A drop-down list action view

For each tab you'd like to add, you must go through the process of requesting a new tab from the action bar, setting the listener, and then adding it to the action bar. **Figure 10.9** shows what the fragment app would look like with tabs for navigating through different content.

Each tab can trigger different events on the fragments within an activity. In the demo example, selecting another tab will switch to a different content fragment.

USING ACTION VIEWS

Action views (like search and menu drop-downs) are somewhat complex and thus are impossible to go into in great detail here. You can use them to add search fields (as there is no longer a hard search button in Honeycomb and beyond) as well as drop-down menus. **Figure 10.10** shows a calendar picker implemented as a drop-down menu on a phone running Ice Cream Sandwich.

For more information on how to make drop-down lists, search fields, and even your own custom views, check out the action bar documentation, at http://developer.android.com/guide/topics/ui/actionbar.html.

WRAPPING UP

As you can see, Google has built user interface paradigms that can be used across all devices. Using the action bar, Google was able to do away with two physical menu buttons (options menu and search), while keeping those concepts active in the user experience. The options menu button was replaced by menu items added to the action bar, and the search button was replaced by the ability to add custom action views to that very same bar.

With fragments, Google has enabled us to place more or less on the screen as the available real estate shifts between devices. Through fragments, we are no longer limited to having one *thing* on the screen at any given time. However, if we need to handle smaller screens, fragments make it easy to shift back into the one-thing-per-screen layout.

Now that you have an understanding of fragments and the action bar, in the next chapter we'll take a look at some useful navigation paradigms that will help you build intuitive applications.

CHAPTER 11

Advanced Navigation

By now, you have just about all the major building blocks necessary to build a basic application. But sometimes, the basic building blocks just aren't fun enough. This chapter gives you a basic overview of two of the most common navigational paradigms, the view pager and the navigation drawer.

THE VIEW PAGER

A view pager is a way of navigating left and right through pages of data, generally using the swipe left and swipe right gestures. A view pager, like a list, takes an adapter, called a PagerAdapter, to generate the content to show. Two subclasses are built into the support library for the PagerAdapter: FragmentPagerAdapter and FragmentStatePagerAdapter. Both essentially accomplish the same thing—they show pages of fragments. Their nuances lie in how they handle non-visible fragments.

FragmentPagerAdapter holds onto in memory each fragment that the user visits, and it keeps the views immediately available for each fragment to the left and right of the visible fragment. This can be memory intensive, so it is more suited for a tab-like navigation where you have only three or four fragments in the adapter.

FragmentStatePagerAdapter holds onto only the savedInstanceState for each fragment visited. This means there will be more overhead when switching back and forth between fragments, but you should be able to page an indefinite number of fragments this way.

In the last chapter, I covered how to add tabs to a fragment; in this one, I'm going to expand on that example and make these tabs swipeable using the ViewPager.

CREATING THE PROJECT

Instead of importing this project from sample code, we are going to use the new project wizard to generate the code, and I'll go over the key parts of what these pieces actually mean.

In Android Studio, select File > New Project; in Eclipse, select File > New > Android Application Project. Give your new project a name, and set the API minimum to 11. Click Next until you get to the screen asking for the name of your activity and your layout. In the Navigation Type menu, select Fixed Tabs + Swipe (in Eclipse) or ActionBar Tabs with ViewPager (in Android Studio). Click Finish. A new project will be created that contains all the boilerplate code for using the view pager. If you run this code as it is, you should see three tabs (**Figure 11.1**).

> **NOTE:** The wizard requires API 11 to generate the ViewPager code, but this is only because it uses the ActionBar. Based on what you learned in Chapter 10, you should have the tools necessary (using AppCompat) to convert this project to be compatible all the way down to version 8 if you need to.

You must be thinking, "This is great! The app is already halfway done!" Well, not quite, but this certainly does provide a great starting point for many projects. Let's dissect the code in the activity and get an idea of what exactly is going on.

FIGURE 11.1 The view pager and action bar tabs from the generated code

ONCREATE

The onCreate of this activity has a lot going on in it, but it is straightforward to follow. The generated code is heavily and helpfully commented, so let's look over it. I've removed the comments for brevity, but the actual code should be similar.

```
@Override
protected void onCreate(Bundle savedInstanceState) {
    super.onCreate(savedInstanceState);
    setContentView(R.layout.activity_main);

    final ActionBar actionBar = getActionBar();
    actionBar.setNavigationMode(ActionBar.NAVIGATION_MODE_TABS);

    mSectionsPagerAdapter = new SectionsPagerAdapter(
            getSupportFragmentManager());
```

```
// Set up the ViewPager with the sections adapter.
mViewPager = (ViewPager) findViewById(R.id.pager);
mViewPager.setAdapter(mSectionsPagerAdapter);

mViewPager.setOnPageChangeListener(new
   ViewPager.SimpleOnPageChangeListener() {
   @Override
   public void onPageSelected(int position) {
      actionBar.setSelectedNavigationItem(position);
   }
});

for (int i = 0; i < mSectionsPagerAdapter.getCount(); i++) {
   actionBar.addTab(actionBar.newTab()
      .setText(mSectionsPagerAdapter.getPageTitle(i))
      .setTabListener(this));
   }
}
```

Aside from the normal setup of the activity using setContentView, the first thing it does is set the ActionBar's navigation mode to ActionBar.NAVIGATION_MODE_TABS. By specifying this, we are letting the ActionBar know that we want to show tabs, and that we want to be able to call tab-related functions. If this is not set, calling functions such as setSelectedNavigationIndex will throw an IllegalStateException, causing your application to crash.

Next, it creates a new class named SectionPagerAdapter. As we will see later, Section PagerAdapter is a custom subclass of FragmentPagerAdapter, which is the class that is primarily responsible for providing fragments to page through.

After creating the adapter, it goes through the familiar process of finding the ViewPager, which is laid out in activity_main.xml, and then setting its adapter with the one we just created. It's similar to the list view in that if you do not set an adapter onto it, no content will be shown.

The last piece of importance here is setting a page change listener. This is where we form a correlation between the action bar tabs and the view pager. This is saying, "when I change pages, change the selected tab to the new page."

The code should look similar to the code in Chapter 10. It's just a simple for-loop adding a number of tabs equal to the number of pages in the adapter.

THE XML

The XML for this activity is simple. Actually, it feels too simple. It has only one item in it, and that is the ViewPager. Remember back in Chapter 3 when we created a view programmatically instead of by using XML? Since this layout has only one view, and its parameters are relatively simple, this might be one of those times that you want to create your layout in XML. Why don't you give it a try?

```
<android.support.v4.view.ViewPager xmlns:android="http://schemas.android.com/
→ apk/res/android"
    android:id="@+id/pager"
    android:layout_width="match_parent"
    android:layout_height="match_parent" />
```

As you can see, all that is being set here is a width, a height, and an ID. What might look different is that ViewPager is prefaced with android.support.v4.view. The ViewPager actually exists only in the support library, and not in the Android framework. Because of this, you have to reference it by its fully qualified name, just as if you were declaring one of your own custom views in XML.

FRAGMENTPAGERADAPTER

The critical piece of the view pager lies within the adapter you supply to it. Creating a ViewPager subclass requires you to override two methods—getItem and getCount—and implement a constructor.

- getItem should return the type of item to be displayed; in this case, a fragment.
- getCount should return the number of items in the adapter. In the example code, it is returning 3, meaning three fragments will be paged through.

In the example code, only one type of fragment is used, but you can use any combination of fragments that you please.

```
public class SectionsPagerAdapter extends FragmentPagerAdapter {
    public SectionsPagerAdapter(FragmentManager fm) {
        super(fm);
    }


    @Override
    public Fragment getItem(int position) {
        Fragment fragment = new DummySectionFragment();
        Bundle args = new Bundle();
        args.putInt(DummySectionFragment.ARG_SECTION_NUMBER,
            position + 1);
        fragment.setArguments(args);
```

```
      return fragment;
    }

    @Override
    public int getCount() {
        // Show 3 total pages.
        return 3;
    }

    @Override
    public CharSequence getPageTitle(int position) {
        Locale l = Locale.getDefault();
        switch (position) {
        case 0:
            String title1 = getString(R.string.title_section1);
            return title1.toUpperCase(l);
        case 1:
            String title2 = getString(R.string.title_section2);
            return title2.toUpperCase(l);
        case 2:
            String title3 = getString(R.string.title_section3);
            return title3.toUpperCase(l);
        }
        return null;
    }
}
```

The getItem function is creating a new fragment for the position that it's passed. getItem is called internally by the FragmentPagerAdapter, and you do not need to call this yourself to show any of the fragments that you wish to display. The example is adding the position as an argument to the fragment so that it can use it to display its position in the fragment's content, but this isn't necessary if you don't want to do it.

Finally, the example overrides a function named getPageTitle. While this isn't required, it's a nice helper function to associate a title with a position in the view pager. If you don't override this, the default implementation will return null, so watch out for NullPointerExceptions.

DUMMYFRAGMENT

DummyFragment is basically just an empty fragment used to demonstrate that the pager holds fragments. Note that fragments can be inner classes and are not required to be a standalone class. This might prove useful for you if you have some fragments that aren't too complex and perform very basic functionality. For example, if a fragment contains only a list and no other logic, it might make sense to have it as an inner class to the activity it's used in, to provide more context into what its purpose is.

That's it! The view pager is a great way to add top-level navigation to your application and add a fun and intuitive way for your users to discover content. As a rule, you should avoid using more than three tabs for your top-level navigation. If you have to go over three tabs, then it might be time to check out the navigation drawer.

THE NAVIGATION DRAWER

The navigation drawer (**Figure 11.2**) is a UI pattern in which a drawer reveals itself from the left side of the screen, either because the user swiped from the left edge of the screen or because they pressed the home icon in the action bar. Users will know that a drawer is available by the presence of three lines next to the home icon. Some designers call this icon the "hamburger" because its three lines look like... well, you get it. **Figure 11.3** shows what the standard three-lined hamburger icon looks like. You can customize this to any icon you'd like, but for convention, make sure it always has three lines.

FIGURE 11.2 The navigation drawer

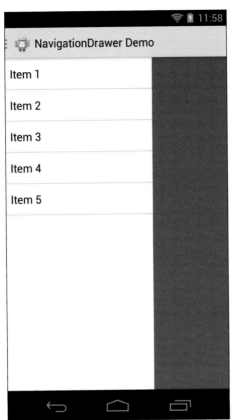

FIGURE 11.3 The navigation drawer's standard icon, sometimes known as the "hamburger"

The contents of the navigation drawer can be any view, but for our demo, we are going to use a list view. The code for this example is a modified example of the drawer demo code on the developer's site, http://developer.android.com/training/implementing-navigation/nav-drawer.html. The official sample code is a great implementation, but for someone not familiar with all the Android APIs, it might be a bit overwhelming. I've removed all the extraneous pieces to demonstrate exactly what is necessary to get a drawer into your application.

ONCREATE

As with all Android projects, onCreate is the best place to figure out what's going on. Let's take a look. Since this is a little longer than the onCreate for the view pager, I'm going to break it into two parts.

```
@Override
protected void onCreate(Bundle savedInstanceState) {
    super.onCreate(savedInstanceState);
    setContentView(R.layout.activity_main);
```

```
mTitle = mDrawerTitle = getTitle();
mDrawerLayout = (DrawerLayout) findViewById(R.id.drawer_layout);

mDrawerList = (ListView) findViewById(R.id.left_drawer);
ArrayAdapter<String> adapter = new ArrayAdapter<String>(this,
    android.R.layout.simple_list_item_1, ITEMS);
mDrawerList.setAdapter(adapter);
mDrawerList.setOnItemClickListener(
  new AdapterView.OnItemClickListener() {
  @Override
  public void onItemClick(AdapterView<?> parent, View view,
      int position, long id) {
    selectItem(position);
  }
});

getSupportActionBar().setDisplayHomeAsUpEnabled(true);
getSupportActionBar().setHomeButtonEnabled(true);
...
```

As usual, we are starting with setContentView to inflate the views for our activity (we will take a look at the XML soon). In our onCreate, we are referencing two views, a Drawer Layout and a ListView. A DrawerLayout is a subclass of ViewGroup, which means that its job is to hold other views. In this case, one of the views that it's holding is the second one we are referencing, a ListView. This ListView is going to act as our navigation menu, and will be what the drawer will show when it is opened.

> **TIP:** You can add a visible shadow to your navigation drawer by calling the setDrawerShadow method of the DrawerLayout with the drawable you'd like to use as a shadow. To use it, you would call the method like this (drawable image is included in the sample project): mDrawerLayout.setDrawerShadow(R.drawable.drawer_shadow, GravityCompat.START);

Just like we did in Chapter 5, we are going to create a simple adapter and set it to our list view. To add interactivity to the list view, let's set an OnItemClickListener and give it a function to select an item. selectItem is a function we are defining ourselves. We'll go into the contents of the select item after we finish onCreate.

Next, we add some flags on the action bar so that it knows what we intend to do with it. setDisplayHomeAsUpEnabled is telling the action bar to show a carrot next to the icon, indicating that pressing the icon will exhibit some sort of "up" or "back" behavior. setHomeButtonEnabled will simply make the home icon clickable.

```
...
mDrawerToggle = new ActionBarDrawerToggle(
    this, mDrawerLayout, R.drawable.ic_drawer,
    R.string.drawer_open, R.string.drawer_close) {

  public void onDrawerClosed(View view) {
    getActionBar().setTitle(mTitle);
  }
  public void onDrawerOpened(View drawerView) {
    getActionBar().setTitle(mDrawerTitle);
  }
};

mDrawerLayout.setDrawerListener(mDrawerToggle);
if (savedInstanceState == null) {
  selectItem(0);
}
}
```

The last part of onCreate is where things start to get interesting. According to the Android documentation, the ActionBarDrawerToggle is "a handy way to tie together the functionality of DrawerLayout and the framework ActionBar to implement the recommended design for navigation drawers."

The ActionBarToggleDrawer takes five arguments, the first three arguably being the most important. Here are the argument descriptions from the online documentation.

- Activity. The activity hosting the drawer.
- DrawerLayout. The drawer layout to link to the given activity's action bar.
- DrawerImageResource. A drawable to use as the drawer indicator (this is the hamburger icon mentioned earlier).
- OpenDrawerContentDescription. A string resource to describe the "open drawer" action for accessibility.
- CloseDrawerContentDescription. A string resource to describe the "close drawer" action for accessibility.

The creation of the ActionBarDrawerToggle is unique in that we are using anonymous inner functions to declare the behavior of the drawer when it is toggled. This is a stylistic choice, and you could very easily create a custom class that extends ActionBarDrawer Toggle. I encourage you to use whichever you feel more comfortable with.

In both onDrawerClosed and onDrawerOpened in our example, we are adjusting the title in the action bar. This is not required, but it is a nice way to give your users a sense of where they are and what they are looking at. When the drawer is open, it should show the title of the drawer in the action bar; when the drawer is closed, it should reflect the content of what the user is looking at.

After initializing ActionBarDrawerToggle, we set it as the listener for our drawer layout. This will make sure that when the drawer toggle is selected, the drawer slides in and out. Now that we have all the pieces set up properly, we set the currently selected item to 0. You will notice that this is wrapped in an if statement that checks whether the saved instance state is null. If it is null, that means that this activity's lifecycle is new. If it isn't null, that means we have some sort of previous state, and we don't want to reinitialize anything.

THE XML

The drawer layout requires a specific setup to work properly. Since it is a child of a view group, its purpose is to hold other views. In a drawer layout, the first view is meant to be the content view, and the second view is meant to be the actual drawer. Setting layout_gravity on the second view is how you set the side of the screen the drawer emerges from. Setting layout_gravity to start will make the drawer emerge from the left side of the screen; setting it to end will make it emerge from the right.

```
<android.support.v4.widget.DrawerLayout
    xmlns:android="http://schemas.android.com/apk/res/android"
    android:id="@+id/drawer_layout"
    android:layout_width="match_parent"
    android:layout_height="match_parent">

    <FrameLayout
        android:id="@+id/content_frame"
        android:layout_width="match_parent"
        android:layout_height="match_parent" />

    <ListView
        android:id="@+id/left_drawer"
        android:layout_width="240dp"
        android:layout_height="match_parent"
        android:layout_gravity="start"
        android:background="#FFF"
        android:divider="#BBB"
        android:dividerHeight="1dp" />

</android.support.v4.widget.DrawerLayout>
```

SWAPPING FRAGMENTS

The navigation drawer is a great way to swap fragments around, and this is exactly what we're doing in our app. The selectItem function that we mentioned earlier (and set to 0) is actually doing all the fragment switching for us.

NOTE: We are writing this function ourselves, which means that we can assign any arbitrary behavior to an item click from the navigation drawer.

```
private void selectItem(int position) {
    // update the main content by replacing fragments
    Fragment fragment = new DummySectionFragment();
    Bundle args = new Bundle();
    args.putInt(DummySectionFragment.ARG_SECTION_NUMBER, position + 1);
    fragment.setArguments(args);

    FragmentManager fragmentManager = getFragmentManager();
    fragmentManager.beginTransaction().replace(
        R.id.content_frame, fragment).commit();

    // update selected item and title, then close the drawer
    setTitle(ITEMS[position]);
    mDrawerLayout.closeDrawer(mDrawerList);
}
```

If this code looks similar to code you've used previously to add fragments, that's because it is! We are creating a new fragment and setting an argument on it, which is used for nothing more than visually displaying which fragment it is.

Next, we use the standard fragment procedure: Get the FragmentManager, begin a transaction, replace a fragment, and commit the change. Done! R.id.content_frame references the frame layout that is located in the activity's XML (mentioned in the previous section).

At the end of these transactions, we are doing a couple of things. First, we are setting the title in the action bar to the item we selected. This will ensure that the title matches the content. After that, we close the drawer as soon as the user selects an item. The user appreciates any extra work you can do for them.

Near the end of the file, you'll notice a couple of functions being overridden, onPost Create and onConfigurationChanged. These are both making state synchronization calls onto ActionBarDrawerToggle. If you're interested in what these calls are actually doing, a quick online search will lead you to the source code. In any case, just remember to add these calls into your activity, and your navigation drawer should behave properly.

WRAPPING UP

Creating interfaces is one of the most enjoyable parts of Android development, and Android has provided some great tools that allow us to quickly create basic applications that use cutting-edge navigation patterns.

In this chapter, you learned how to use the new project wizard to build an application that already has an action bar with tabs and a view pager, and you learned about all the pieces that were generated.

You also checked out what the navigation drawer is all about. Although there is a lot you can do with a navigation drawer, there isn't much code necessary to get it working.

From the basic view all the way up to the complex fragment, and from simple network requests to fully functional background services, you have all the tools you need to create just about any application you can imagine. Take some time to play around with all the examples we've created thus far, because in the next chapter, we're going to upload one of these applications onto the Google Play Store so that anyone can download it! (Or no one, whichever you prefer.)

CHAPTER 12

Publishing Your Application

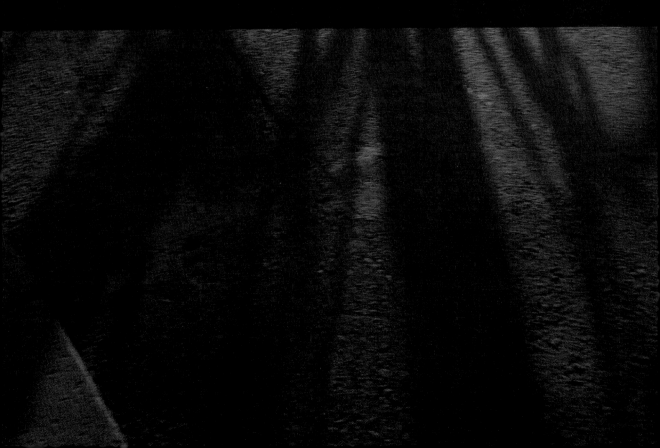

For the most part, the Google Play Store is one of the easiest-to-use application stores I've ever encountered. But although you can update an application almost instantly without any of the hassles of other app stores, there are still a few things you should be aware of before you publish. We'll cover packaging, versioning, and creating a release build.

PACKAGING AND VERSIONING

There are a few key points in your manifest that you need to pay attention to before you consider producing a release build to go to market. You'll need to make sure your application isn't debuggable (not so much an issue with newer versions of the Android client). You'll also want to make sure your package name is unique and consistent in each subsequent version. Last, there are two values to pay attention to when upgrading an existing application.

PREVENTING DEBUGGING

Shipping your application out the door with debugging enabled will allow anyone who can connect their phone to their computer to enable debugging and step through lines of code in your app, look at the contents of variables, and do other things that no security-aware engineer would like to have happen. The debugging flag is turned off by default, but if you've turned it on, it will appear in the application portion of the manifest:

```
<application
    android:icon="@drawable/ic_launcher"
    android:label="@string/app_name"
    android:debuggable="true">
```

When the application ships, make sure that you either remove the line entirely or set the following:

```
android:debuggable="false"
```

NAMING THE PACKAGE

The package you declare in your manifest can, for the most part, contain almost any string you fancy. I've highlighted one from a previous example here:

```
<?xml version="1.0" encoding="utf-8"?>
<manifest xmlns:android="http://schemas.android.com/apk/res/android"
    package="com.peachpit.layouts"
    android:versionCode="1"
    android:versionName="1.0">
```

Although I named this package to correspond to my layouts example, you could just as easily declare a package like

```
package="com.sparkle.pants.fairy.dust.unicorn"
```

I wouldn't recommend using the unicorn example (it's somewhat outrageous), but the fact remains that you can. However, the package name you choose must be different from all other existing packages in the entire Google Play Store. Be sure it's unique and that it's something you can live with for as long as you upgrade the application. When you upgrade your app, it absolutely must have the same package name as the build that came before it. Typically, the naming convention goes something like com.company_name.product_name. But again, the package name for your application is entirely up to you.

VERSIONING

There are two values to pay attention to when updating an existing application. First, you should (but are not required to) increase the value inside the versionName field of the manifest declaration. Standard rules for the version number apply: Major releases get a new primary number (1.0 to 2.0), while small patches should get a secondary bump (1.0 to 1.1). The version name is what shows to the user in the Play Store and in your application's details screen. The version name is "1.0" in the previous example's manifest file.

The field you *must* pay careful attention to is versionCode. This is the value that must change every time you do an update for the Play Store. Sending an update to the Play Store will be rejected unless you change the versionCode. Typically, Android developers will make the version code by taking the periods out of the version name and padding each portion of the name to create a two-digit number for each section. The number must be unique, but it does not necessarily have to be sequential. So version 1.0.1 would become 010001, and 2.3.12 would become 020312. This is a basic way to make sure your version names stay tied to the version code without much complexity. It's a good idea to make this number constantly grow even though, according to the documentation, it isn't technically required to. However, adopting a convention of incrementing the numbers ensures it will be unique.

SETTING A MINIMUM SDK VALUE

Google Play requires that you specify a minimum SDK value for your application. You can do this in the manifest by including the uses-sdk field, like so:

```
<?xml version="1.0" encoding="utf-8"?>
<manifest xmlns:android="http://schemas.android.com/apk/res/android"
    package="com.haseman.location"
    android:versionCode="1"
    android:versionName="1.0">
    <uses-sdk android:minSdkVersion="10"/>
    <!-- The rest of your application goes here-->
</manifest>
```

The number in minSdkVersion corresponds to the integer value for the SDK. In this case, by declaring version 10, I'm not allowing phones earlier than Android 2.3.3 (which is SDK version 10) to install my application. Be sure to test your application on the versions you support, even if you just test it briefly with an emulator.

PACKAGING AND SIGNING

So your version number is sorted, your code is tested, and all your resources are in place—it's time to make a release build before submitting.

There are a few ways you can go about producing your final APK, depending on the IDE you're using: Apache's Ant (which will build your application from the command line in conjunction with the build.xml file), Eclipse's Android Build tools, Android Studio's Build tools, or the Gradle command line. If you want to build your Eclipse project with the command line, head on over to http://developer.android.com/tools/building/building-cmdline.html; it's a wonderfully comprehensive guide to building with Ant. If you built your project in Android Studio and want to build from the command line, see Chapter 13, where I'll go into how to modify your Gradle file and run through the Gradle commands. In this chapter, however, I'll be focusing on creating your release build through your IDE.

EXPORTING A SIGNED BUILD

The IDE tools make it very easy to produce an effective release build. If you're using Eclipse, simply right-click your project in the Package Explorer and choose Android Tools > Export Signed Application Package (**Figure 12.1**). If you're using Android Studio, choose Build > Generate Signed APK (**Figure 12.2**).

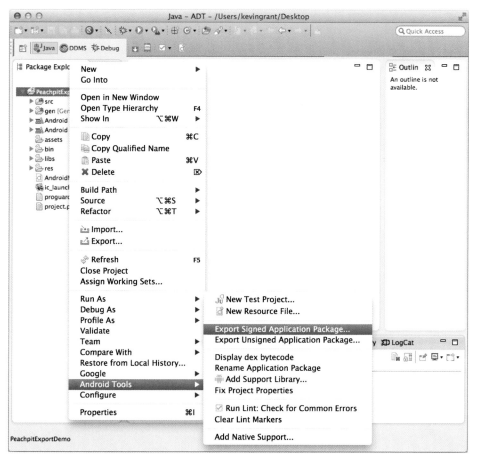

FIGURE 12.1 Exporting a release build in Eclipse

FIGURE 12.2 Exporting a release build in Android Studio

FIGURE 12.3 Creating a keystore file in Eclipse

FIGURE 12.4 Creating a keystore file in Android Studio

REMEMBER TO DISABLE LOGGING

Before you ship anything, run through your code base and make sure there are no extra logging lines that you don't want anyone with a micro USB cable to see. Remember, too, that applications with the right permissions can view log output. That said, shipping your application with some logging in place for catastrophic errors isn't a bad idea (in case there are failures in the field).

You'll be asked if you want to use an existing keystore file or create a new one. Because this is your first time releasing your product, you'll need to create a new one.

In Eclipse, enter a location for the file, or click the Browse button to find one. Enter a password, and re-enter it to confirm that it is correctly typed (**Figure 12.3**).

In Android Studio, click the Create New button in the dialog (**Figure 12.4**).

The *keystore* is a file that can contain any number of keys. For your purposes, you'll really need only one key. All your applications can be signed with the same one, or you can use different keys—it's up to you (but I recommend using only one, because it's less to keep track of).

Once you've created your keystore, your IDE will ask you to create a key. You aren't required to fill in all the lower fields. For guidance, check out **Figure 12.5** for Eclipse, or **Figure 12.6** for Android Studio.

You'll be creating a key (to place in your new keystore file) that requires an alias and its own password.

FIGURE 12.5 Creating a key in Eclipse

FIGURE 12.6 Creating a key in Android Studio

BACKING UP YOUR KEYSTORE FILE

I'll say it again: **Back up your keystore file**. If I could invent a way to make an HTML `<blink>` tag in a printed book, I would do it here. The Play Store will not let you upgrade an application if you haven't signed it with the same key. If you lose the keystore file you've just created, you'll never be able to upgrade your application. Burn it to a disk, and store the disk somewhere other than your house. Save it in the cloud (Amazon S3, Dropbox, your mother's house) in as many safe places as you can.

Be sure that you make the number you use for the Validity field large enough to be valid for a very, very long time. You never know, Android could still be around a thousand years from now. It pays to be prepared. Last, you'll need to fill out at least one of the several remaining fields, but I recommend you fill in as many as apply.

Click Next (or OK, in Android Studio) to create your key. You'll just need to tell your IDE where to put your APK, and you're finished!

SUBMITTING YOUR BUILD

At this point, it's time to sign up for a developer account and submit your build. Android's application submission page is fairly self-explanatory, but I should point out that it's important to provide the Play Store with as many screenshots, videos, and graphical assets as you have time to generate. Making the decision to purchase an application can be a difficult one. Users need to be able to trust that your application actually works as advertised, so giving them a sneak peek is essential.

WATCH YOUR CRASH REPORTS AND FIX THEM

The marketplace provides a very helpful capability: Users, when they experience a crash, have the option of reporting that crash to you (**Figure 12.7**). Take advantage of it as much as possible. Get in touch with users, and fix absolutely everything you can. When you get stuck, go online and use every resource available (your favorite search engine, Google Groups, or Stack Overflow, to name a few). If you're seeing a crash you don't understand, chances are high that other developers have battled the same thing; we're a very helpful bunch.

UPDATE FREQUENTLY

Your application, after you submit it, will show up in the Play Store within a few hours, and within a day you will start seeing installation statistics (**Figure 12.8**). This allows you to frequently update in order to add small features, fix bugs, and make small tweaks. No other platform allows you this kind of speed from submission to availability. Use it. You'll be amazed by how grateful your users will be if you respond to their problems quickly.

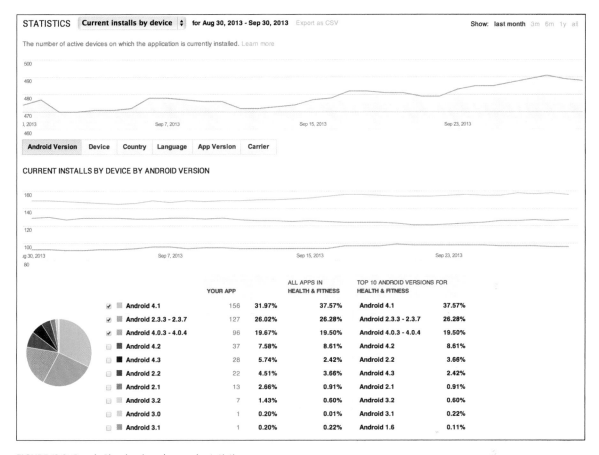

FIGURE 12.8 Google Play developer's console statistics

WRAPPING UP

Before we move on to the last chapter, which covers Gradle, I want to give you one more piece of advice: Make a meaningful contribution to the Android landscape. While you'll undoubtedly have questions that this book cannot answer, you now have the vocabulary and knowledge that will allow you to find answers. This means you have no excuse but to make something amazing. Please—the Play Store is, for lack of a better phrase, full of crap. The world doesn't need another flatulence app; we need things that make data more accessible, meaningful, fun, useful, and interesting. Do not build apps, build applications.

Good luck, and happy hacking.

CHAPTER 13

Gradle, the New Build System

If you've been working through all the chapters using Android Studio—or if you have been working in Eclipse and have been wondering what this new build system is all about—this chapter aims to answer some of the questions you might have. While Gradle is different from any of the Java and Android programming we have dealt with before, it will prove to be a handy tool in your arsenal for creating a new generation of Android applications.

Gradle is an existing build system that Android has adopted to replace its previous build system. Gradle creates a unified build experience between the IDE and the command line. In its current form, Eclipse has a different build system from Ant, meaning that the things you can do in Ant don't always translate to things that you can build from Eclipse. Android Studio was built with Gradle in mind, and when you make changes to the Gradle file, Android Studio will respect those changes and will always exhibit the same behavior whether built from the command line or directly in the IDE.

ANATOMY OF A GRADLE FILE

As you've come to expect, each new project will be generated with two Gradle files: a top-level Gradle file, to which you can add configurations to be used on all projects in the folder; and an inner Gradle file, which contains information for building the specific project that it's located in. Since nearly all cases of using your build file will be on the inner Gradle file, that's the one we are going to focus on. Go ahead and create a new project in Android Studio, or open an existing one, and let's take a look. This inner Gradle file is located in `<ProjectName>/<ProjectName>/src/build.gradle`.

```
buildscript {
    repositories {
        mavenCentral()
    }
    dependencies {
        classpath 'com.android.tools.build:gradle:0.6.+'
    }
}
apply plugin: 'android'

repositories {
    mavenCentral()
}

android {
    compileSdkVersion 18
    buildToolsVersion "18.1.0"

    defaultConfig {
        minSdkVersion 8
        targetSdkVersion 16
    }
}

dependencies {
    compile 'com.android.support:appcompat-v7:18.0.0'
}
```

Your new project should look something like the code above. Let's dive into this build file to understand exactly what's going on.

BUILDSCRIPT AND PLUG-INS

The top of every Android Gradle file should contain the `buildscript`, which contains two fields—repositories and dependencies—that contain information about which repository to fetch Gradle from and which version of Gradle to use. In most cases, you will be using `mavenCentral` as your repository, and you'll use whatever version of Gradle that the new project wizard chooses for you.

When the Gradle version says `0.6.+`, the + tells the build system to use whatever the highest level of Gradle version 6 is on the system. If 6.2 is available, it will use that; if 6.3 is available, it will use that, and so on. This prevents you from having to modify your build file in between minor releases of the build system. This section should rarely have to be modified. It only needs to be updated if you wish to change major versions of the build system; for instance, changing from 0.6.+ to 0.7.+.

```
buildscript {
    repositories {
        mavenCentral()
    }
    dependencies {
        classpath 'com.android.tools.build:gradle:0.6.+'
    }
}
apply plugin: 'android'

repositories {
    mavenCentral()
}
```

Below the `buildscript` is `apply plugin: 'android'`, which tells Gradle that you intend to use the Android plug-in to build your project. This is a key line in case you ever want to build an Android library project. In which case, you replace `android` with `android-library`, letting Gradle know to build this as a library instead of as an APK. Android library projects (known as .aar files) are a great way to distribute library code containing Android-specific classes and resources. They are an advanced subject and out of scope for our purposes, but it's worth knowing they exist.

Lastly, `repositories` appears again, because we can fetch libraries from a source other than where we retrieve Gradle from. As you might expect, in most cases you'll never have to modify this, but it's good to know that you can.

THE ANDROID STUFF

Finally we arrive at the Android-specific stuff, the things that we are all comfortable with by now. The primary purpose of this portion of the build file is to tell Gradle which versions of Android we want to build our project with. Ideally, this information should match the values set in your AndroidManifest.xml file.

```
android {
    compileSdkVersion 18
    buildToolsVersion "18.1.0"

    defaultConfig {
        minSdkVersion 8
        targetSdkVersion 16
    }
}
```

- **compileSdkVersion.** The version of Android that your application will be compiled with. As when creating a new project, this should be set to the newest version of Android that you can support.
- **buildToolsVersion.** The version of the build tools to use. This has the chance to become outdated as you update your Android SDK over time. Keep an eye on your build tools version when using the SDK Manager, and update this value accordingly.
- **minSdkVersion.** Used for filtering your application in Google Play. Only devices running at least the minimum version supported will be able to search for and download the application.
- **targetSdkVersion.** The version of Android you designed the application for. This has an impact on various compatibility features that are enabled, so set this to the highest SDK possible so that you are never caught by surprise by the compatibility features that are enabled. For example, if you set your target SDK version to 11 (Honeycomb), all your EditTexts and ProgressBars will look as if they are on a version 11 device, even when it's running something newer.

At the end of your Gradle file, depending on whether you selected some of the optional libraries (such as the support modes) when creating your project, you will see a section for dependencies. This is where some of Gradle's great flexibility comes in, allowing you to add libraries easily and seamlessly to your project.

```
dependencies {
    compile 'com.android.support:appcompat-v7:18.0.0'
}
```

If you've been using Android Studio in the prior chapters, then you're already vaguely familiar with this process. In this area, you can add new libraries, library projects, Java JAR files, and even locally added .aar files. After you add or remove a library, just select Tools > Android > Sync Project with Gradle Files to update your project to reflect the new configurations.

BUILD TYPES

Now that you have a general understanding of the different parts of a Gradle file, let's see how to take it a step further and do some interesting things.

Build types is a concept that allows you different build configurations of a specific build. By default, Gradle uses two types—debug and release—but you can add as many types as you see fit for your purposes. In the following code, you can see where we are referencing the two default variants as well as adding our own third variant, named customType.

```
buildTypes {
    debug {
        ...
    }
    release {
        ...
    }
    customType {
        ...
    }
}
```

After adding the variants you wish, sync your project with the Gradle file, and the variants you added will be available for you to work with. In the lower-left corner of Android Studio, you can click the Build Variant tab (**Figure 13.1**), which will show you all the variants available to you. If you select one, Android Studio will install this variant onto your device or emulator when you run it.

FIGURE 13.1 Select the build type you would like to run.

You might want to use a custom build type if you want a debug build that uses a different debug URL for your application's content, or if you are making a different release build for different Android marketplaces, such as a release build for Google Play and a release build for the Amazon Appstore.

Another great feature of build types is their ability to programmatically affect the application at build time, thus allowing things like giving debug versions a different package name. This is particularly useful because it allows a debug version and a release version to be installed side by side.

```
android {
    compileSdkVersion 18
    buildToolsVersion "18.1.0"

    defaultConfig {
        minSdkVersion 8
        targetSdkVersion 16
    }

    buildTypes {
        debug {
            packageNameSuffix ".debug"
            versionNameSuffix ".debug"
        }
    }
}
```

Property Name	Default value in DSL object	Default value
versionCode	-1	value from manifest if present
versionName	null	value from manifest if present
minSdkVersion	-1	value from manifest if present
targetSdkVersion	-1	value from manifest if present
packageName	null	value from manifest if present
testPackageName	null	app package name + ".test"
testInstrumentationRunner	null	android.test.InstrumentationTestRunner
signingConfig	null	null
proguardFile	N/A (set only)	N/A (set only)
proguardFiles	N/A (set only)	N/A (set only)

FIGURE 13.2 Build type options you can override

As the highlighted code suggests, .debug will be added to both the package name and the version name, and this doesn't require further modification to any other code in your project to make it work. **Figure 13.2** shows all the options that can be overridden in the build types.

ADDING VALUES TO BUILDCONFIG

BuildConfig is a class generated by Android that contains information determined at build time. Previously, we have been able to use only BuildConfig to determine if the build you were running was a debug build, by checking the BuildConfig.DEBUG variable. This has limited usage. But with Gradle, we can add our own variables to BuildConfig. For example, let's say you want to have a different logging tag for debug versions than for release versions. You could do this by checking the BuildConfig.DEBUG flag, but instead let's add a variable to BuildConfig.

```
buildTypes {
    debug {
        packageNameSuffix ".debug"
        versionNameSuffix ".debug"
        buildConfig "public static final String TAG = \"DEBUG\";"
    }
    release {
        buildConfig "public static final String TAG = \"RELEASE\";"
    }
}
```

With these lines in your file, you can reference BuildConfig.TAG to get the appropriate tag, depending on whether it's a release build or a debugging build. The buildConfig property is adding this string to the build file, which means that quotation marks need to be escaped, and if you want to add multiple properties, they are all added onto this one buildConfig. Here is what it would look like if you wanted to add multiple properties:

```
buildConfig "public static final String TAG = \"RELEASE\";" +
"public static final int AUTHORITY = \"content://com.peachpit.release\";"
```

PRODUCT FLAVORS

Product flavors are similar to build types in that they give you a different way of building your application; they are dissimilar in that they allow you to go further with build customization and add different source code and assets, depending on the build type. For example, let's say you have an application that has a free version and a paid version. You could accomplish this with a build type by setting some `buildConfig` flags and adding a special .free or .paid suffix to your package name. But what if you want to change the application icon? Or, what if you want to add more graphics or code for the paid version? That's where a flavor really starts to shine.

You can define a new flavor by adding a `productFlavors` section in the `android` section of your build file.

```
android {
    compileSdkVersion 18
    buildToolsVersion "17"

    defaultConfig {
        minSdkVersion 8
        targetSdkVersion 18
    }

    productFlavors{
        free {
            packageName "com.peachpit.free"
        }

        paid {
            packageName "com.peachpit.paid"
        }
    }
}
```

With the product flavors defined in the manifest file, you can now add different source folders for them. For each flavor you want to support, you can add a new source directory in *<ProjectName>*/*<ProjectName>*/src/*<FlavorName>*. This directory will directly mimic the src/main folder for everything you would like to replace. If you would like a different application icon for your free version, then you can add it in *flavorName*/res/drawable-xhdpi/ic_launcher.png. The file must have the same name and be located in the same path location as where the original is located, or else it will not be properly overridden. **Figure 13.3** shows the potential project structure supporting our two flavors and overriding the launcher icon. It's important to note that all flavors will be based on the `main` source folder, differing only where you override the files.

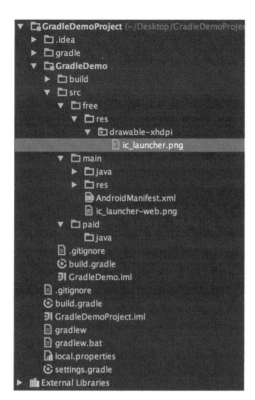

FIGURE 13.3 Project with separate source folders for flavors

BUILD VARIANTS

Now that you know what you can accomplish with build types and product flavors, let's bring them together to explain the concept of a build variant. A *build variant* is the combination of flavors and types. It is probably best explained by referring back to the Build Variants tab in the lower-left corner of Android Studio. Before we do that, go ahead and modify your build.gradle (located in *<project name>*/*<project name>*/build.gradle) to have the following types and flavors.

```
android {
  buildTypes{
    debug {
    }

    release {
    }

    amazon {
    }
```

FIGURE 13.4 Each
product flavor builds
each of the build types,
resulting in a build
variant.

```
    }
    productFlavors{
        free {
        }
        paid {
        }
    }
}
```

After syncing your Gradle file, check out the Build Variant tab. Click the Build Variant drop-down in the tab, and you should see six options. The relationship between build types and product flavors should now be immediately obvious (**Figure 13.4**). Each product flavor will build all of the different build types. This means that the example code will have debug, release, and Amazon builds for both your paid and free versions.

SIGNING AND BUILDING

One of the last key pieces to building your applications for release is adding your signing key to the build file. There are many way to accomplish this, but one of the simplest is to add a signingConfig section to your build file.

```
android {
    signingConfigs {
        release {
            storeFile file("my-release-key.keystore")
            storePassword "****"
```

```
        keyAlias "****"
        keyPassword "****"
      }
    }
}
```

This keystore can be the same keystore we generated for publishing our application to Google Play from Chapter 12, "Publishing Your Application," or it can be a new one. Refer back to Chapter 12 if you need a refresher on how to generate one. By adding this, you are saying "use this signing key when generating the release build type." Be careful when you're adding your credentials to this file; you want to make sure that you don't accidentally commit your keystore's password and other information to your version control system.

With everything in place, the last thing you need to do is run the following command from the root directory of your project:

`./gradlew build`

gradlew stands for Gradle Wrapper, and build will kick off all the tasks necessary to build all the variants in your project. After the build is finished, you'll find all of your APKs in the *<projectName>*/*<projectName>*/build/apk folder of your project, and all of them will be named appropriately for their product flavor and build type.

WRAPPING UP

I've covered only the tip of the iceberg of what is possible using the new Gradle build system. Pulling in specific versions of libraries, modifying build variables to be referenced in your projects, and creating your own build variants are just some of the things that were never possible before. If you want to explore more, read the official Gradle Plugin User Guide, located at http://tools.android.com/tech-docs/new-build-system/user-guide, where you will find a lot of the information provided in this chapter, plus so much more.

By following along through this chapter, you are leaps and bounds ahead of the game because you understand the basics of how Gradle works. As the Gradle plug-in for Android continues to evolve, you will have a better understanding of how the pieces are supposed to fit together, and you'll be at the forefront of the Android build technology.

INDEX

NUMBERS

SYMBOL

A

M

main menu
- ArrayAdapter, 108
- creating data, 104–105
- example, 109
- ListActivity, 105–106, 109
- reacting to click events, 108–109

main thread
- ANR (App Not Responding) crash, 85–86
- AsyncTask abstract task, 89–93
- best practices, 86
- considering for services, 125
- getting back to, 88
- getting off, 87–88
- IntentService, 94–99
- Loader class, 100
- managing, 84–85
- verifying, 86

manifest files
- AndroidManifest.xml, 24
- android:name, 45
- for maps, 183

manifest registration, 37–38

map view
- CameraUpdates, 187–188
- MarkerOptions, 187–188
- running, 187–188

MapFragment component
- adding to manifest, 183
- creating, 184–185
- described, 181
- getting, 181–183
- modifying, 184

maps. *See also* locations
- adding to manifest, 183
- adjusting activity, 184
- API key, 185
- FragmentActivity, 184
- SDK manager options, 181

MarkerOptions, using with maps, 187–188

marshaling process, explained, 134

match_parent definition, 67

media. *See also* movies
- loading data, 160–161
- OnDestroy method, 161
- onErrorListener, 161
- playing, 160–161

media players, cleanup, 174

MediaPlayer states
- Idle, 162
- Initialized, 162
- Playing, 162
- Prepared, 162

MediaScanner, using, 159

menu. *See* main menu

menu items
- adding to action bar, 205–206
- reacting to clicks, 206–208

menu list item, creating, 107. *See also* ListActivity

<merge> tag, using with layout folders, 147

messages, sending toasts, 41

movie playback process, 156

movies. *See also* media
- adding VideoView, 156
- getting media to play, 157–159
- passing URIs to video view, 159
- setting up VideoView, 157

moving data, 43–45

music
- binding to music service, 165
- cursor loader, 166
- finding recent tracks, 165–167
- Idle state, 162
- Initialized state, 162
- Loader class, 168–169
- longer-running, 164
- MediaPlayer and state, 162
- playing sound effects, 163
- playing sounds, 162–163
- Playing state, 162
- Prepared state, 162

views (*continued*)

    wrap_content definition, 53

    WRAP_CONTENT definition, 53

    in XML, 50–51

virtual device emulator

    Snapshot option, 12

    troubleshooting, 21

    Use Host GPU option, 12

    using, 9–12

visibility, changing for views, 55–58

W

width and height, determining for views, 51, 53

Windows

    installing Android Studio, 6

    installing Eclipse (ADT Bundle), 5

working devices. *See also* devices

    limiting access to, 149–151

    SDK version number, 150

    <uses> tag, 150

X

XML

    AbsoluteLayout, 68–70

    custom views, 61–62

    editing, 28

    vs. Java layouts, 55

    match_parent definition, 53

    navigation drawer, 221

    showing fragments, 194–197

    view pager, 215

    views in, 50–51

    wrap_content definition, 53

XML files

    packed binary format, 63

    referencing resources, 63

XML terms

    dip or dp (device-independent pixels), 67

    match_parent definition, 67

    px (pixels), 67